Praise for *In My Grandmother's House*

"In this gripping and authentic text, Dr. Yolanda Pierce teaches us to listen with radical attentiveness, uncovering the analytical brilliance, courageous sacrifice, and definitive theology of her grandmother. As she excavates the intergenerational recipes and patterns out of which her own life is created, she gives the reader access to deep wells of faith and wisdom. This text is a love letter to Black grandmothers and a show way quilt for young people. It is essential reading for all who hear the whisper of the still, small voice and feel unsure of how to respond."

—Melissa Harris-Perry, journalist, speaker, and professor at Wake Forest University

"Within the pages of *In My Grandmother's House*, Dr. Yolanda Pierce brings to the forefront the titans of faith formation, the holders of theological wisdom, the guides who rarely receive credit from the academy for having crafted a faith that endures: Black grandmothers. By giving language to the ways Black women have long helped us make sense of the Divine, Dr. Pierce offers us a window into the sacred lives of Black women, at once centering ourselves, our histories, and our God."

—Austin Channing Brown, *New York Times* bestselling author of *I'm Still Here*

"From the opening sentence to the closing paragraph, Dr. Yolanda Pierce provides a spiritual meal we did not know we desperately needed as a community of joyous believers and wounded family members who occupy the space we call the Black church. Dr. Pierce becomes this generation's spiritual *griot*; her powerful storytelling challenges, inspires, and demands we hold the brokenness and the blessedness of the space we call the Black church in both hands. She pushes us to refuse to release the sweet and sour flavors mixed in the beautiful pot of our Black spirituality framed by the womanist power of our grandmothers. Thank you, Dr. Pierce, for being a brilliant, radical, and loving truth-teller."

—Rev. Dr. Otis Moss III, author, activist, and senior pastor of Trinity United Church of Christ

"I used to think talking about Black life, or even Black faith, was about convincing white people to be better. But that's far too limiting. It is about giving us words, setting our bodies free, living in ways that allow us to feel seen, inspired, protected. It is about deep love, a deep faith in the possibility of better for ourselves and our country. Dr. Yolanda Pierce does just that: she welcomes us into the sacred space between Black bodies, God, kitchens, living rooms, sanctuaries, cities, and classrooms. . . . This is a book that is both brilliantly told and beautifully written—a book you will want to read, read again, talk about, sing about, cry with, hold onto, and be held by."

—Danté Stewart, writer, speaker, and activist

"Dr. Yolanda Pierce gives us the gift of inviting us into the faith of her grandmother, and so many others who have gone before. For those of us born entrenched in white patriarchal Christianity, this gift is profound. In her poetic, theologically rich reflections on growing up in the Black church, Dr. Pierce invites our gaze to honor the women who have upheld a profound yet overlooked aspect of American Christianity. This is a wonderful introduction to womanist theology that is life-giving and nurturing even as it invites constant reflection on the part of the reader."

—D. L. Mayfield, author of *The Myth of the American Dream* and *Assimilate or Go Home*

"*In My Grandmother's House* is profoundly hopeful, deeply challenging, and always surprising in the best sense. Through the stories of her grandmother and the older Black women in the church, Dr. Yolanda Pierce offers a powerful vision of a God who loves Black women and is deeply invested in their wholeness and freedom. This work of womanist theology is for *everyone* because it offers a theological lens for the liberation work Black women have always engaged in—it calls us to take Jesus out of the box of tradition so we can see the subversive work of God in the world. After reading it, I wanted to live in her grandmother's house and glean her wisdom and love for God. *In My Grandmother's House* is a gift that will inspire and change you—it's a must-read!"

—Karen González, author of *The God Who Sees*

"Dr. Pierce speaks to all of our hearts by testifying of the goodness of the Black church through her grandmother theology and stories of Black women of faith. This intellectual and emotional masterpiece is just the healing balm we need in a world deprived of the unconditional love and wisdom of Black grandmothers."

—Khristi Lauren Adams, author of *Parable of the Brown Girl*

IN MY GRANDMOTHER'S HOUSE

IN MY GRANDMOTHER'S HOUSE

Black Women, Faith,
and the Stories We Inherit

YOLANDA PIERCE

Broadleaf Books

Minneapolis

IN MY GRANDMOTHER'S HOUSE
Black Women, Faith, and the Stories We Inherit

Excerpt from "Making Foots" from *Rice: Poems* by Nikki Finney (Evanston, IL: TriQuarterly Books, 2013). Copyright © 2013 by Nikki Finney. Reprinted by permission of Northwestern University Press.

"Nazarene." Copyright © 1970 by the Pauli Murray Foundation, from DARK TESTAMENT AND OTHER POEMS by Pauli Murray. Used by permission of Liveright Publishing Corporation.

Cover Image: Sidhe/istock
Cover design: Love Arts

Print ISBN: 978-1-5064-6471-8
eBook ISBN: 978-1-5064-6472-5

In my Father's house are many mansions: if it were not so, I would have told you. I go to prepare a place for you. And if I go and prepare a place for you, I will come again, and receive you unto myself; that where I am, there ye may be also. And whither I go ye know, and the way ye know.

—JOHN 14:2-4

In my grandmother's house, there were biscuits, and hymns, and stories. In my grandmother's church, there was preaching, and joy, and firm rebuke. The faith my grandmother taught me has prepared me for this place. And the faith I have shaped into my own will prepare me for the next. I do not fear the world that is to come, knowing that heaven may be a storefront church or apartment living room where the saints of God are gathered home, telling the story of how they've overcome, knowing we will all understand it better by and by.

—YOLANDA PIERCE

For the remnant,
living in the tension between the contradictions
and the beauty of their faith

Contents

Preface

For I received from the Lord that which I also delivered to you.

—1 Corinthians 11:23

I am a daughter of an imperfect thing we call the Black church. I love that imperfect thing with all my own imperfections, brokenness, and flaws. I love it enough to have committed a lifetime and a career to loving her people and telling her stories. That imperfect church has loved me, chastised me, and strengthened me. And the tradition of the elders that I have received, even when I challenge it, has given my life meaning and joy. My generation may be the last remnant of a tradition that is quickly fading away: a Holy Ghost–filled, foot-stomping, tambourine-playing, chicken-frying-in-the-basement, aisle-running, all-night-tarrying, sanctified, down-home, unapologetically saved tradition. In an era of megachurches, celebrity pastors, ten-thousand-seat sanctuaries, and state-of-the-art video productions, the tradition of my particular church elders is rapidly fading away. And I am left to wonder: How can I best remember and honor all that they have sown in me, and others, for generations?

Parádosis, a Greek term appearing in the Bible, is often translated as "the tradition of the elders." Explicitly, it was the orally transmitted wisdom, teaching, and doctrine that was passed from generation to generation. In the Gospel of Matthew, the Pharisees rebuke Jesus and his disciples for transgressing the "tradition of the elders" when the disciples fail to wash their hands before eating. The Pharisees could not reconcile some of the new teachings of Jesus with what they had learned from the elders, doctrine they had been taught all their life.

I know this struggle well. Every day I attempt to write, live, and remember the traditions and wisdom I have received from my elders even as I wrestle with the new lessons my faith teaches me. We often live in the tension—both agreement and disagreement—between what the elders have taught us and what walking with Jesus reveals.

This book is my attempt to retrieve the religious legacy I have inherited and keep it alive for those who are still to come. I am formally trained as a scholar of religion and literature, and I am a womanist theologian. Womanism is a term coined by African American writer Alice Walker and adapted by Black women theologians: those of us who did not see our lives reflected in the theology being written by either white or Black men nor in the feminist theology written by white women. Womanist theologians have created a space to tell our stories and craft a liberating theology. While the lessons of womanist theology are not exclusive to Black women, they are informed by how Black women have to show up in the world—how race and class and gender and sexual identity and social location shape our theological viewpoints. I cannot divorce my faith from the realities of living in the body of a Black woman, born in a country whose original sin is racism.

More importantly, this book is a work of grandmother theology, a subset of womanist thought. Grandmother theology is rooted in generational wisdom, in the way that time and age and maturity provide an alternative lens through which to know and understand God. In a world eager to promote the newest wunderkind, grandmother theology carries us two or more generations back: to the kitchens, hair salons, gardens, and church basements of older Black women who are often invisible in theological discourse but without whom the American Christian church would cease to exist. I had a praying grandmother, and nothing I have accomplished would have been possible without her prayers.

I recall the very first time I officiated at the Communion table. I was the embodiment of so many impossibilities: An ordained minister, but a woman who grew up in a denomination that did not ordain women. A tenured professor, but the first in my family to attend college. A Black Christian, but a scholar of how doctrinal Christianity shaped white supremacy. As I spoke the instituting words—"For I received from the Lord that which I also delivered to you"—I was overwhelmed by the multiple meanings of these simple words. What I had received from the Lord went beyond the elements of the Communion table and the salvation it celebrated. What I had received, and what this book shares with you, are the stories of a faith, birthed in a Brooklyn storefront church and nurtured by the elders who loved me, prayed for me, and set my feet on a solid foundation.

1 There Is a Name

I know only that his name / Reveals that gift of pain / That only love can bear.

—Pauli Murray, "Nazarene"

In my grandmother's house, the religion was real and tangible. In my grandmother's house, Jesus was a Black man. Despite the habits of others of their generation, born right after the Great Depression, my grandparents never displayed a picture of white Jesus. They never hung a portrait of a man with blond hair, blue eyes, and a golden halo, like the pictures I glimpsed at my friends' houses or saw in the stained-glass windows of even some African American churches. There was never a picture of the white Jesus at Leonardo da Vinci's *The Last Supper* gracing our walls, nor was there an image of white Jesus holding a lamb anywhere in our house.

The Jesus I remember, whose picture was hanging on the wall alongside those of Martin Luther King Jr. and Malcolm X, was a Black man. Amateur artist unknown, this picture was of a Jesus with burnished skin, curly hair, piercing brown eyes, and an angry look. Years later, when I read James Baldwin's description of Jesus as a "disreputable, sun-baked Hebrew," my mind took me back to the picture that hung in my grandparents' living room. This Black Jesus wasn't lowly, meek, or mild. He had no use for carrying around lambs. He wore a crown of thorns instead of a golden halo, and his hair was a curly Afro or twisted locs instead of golden tresses. This childhood image of Black Jesus left such a powerful impression that even today, when I look into the eyes of the Black men in my life, I see the face of Jesus looking back at me.

I never learned how my grandfather, born on a former tobacco plantation in North Carolina, or my grandmother, born on a former cotton plantation in Georgia, came to know, love, and display a Black Jesus. They would have been surrounded by images of divine whiteness. Almost every book, prayer card, tract, Bible, and piece of popular culture they, as deeply pious Christians, would have been acquainted with would have depicted Jesus as white. I've long wondered how they resisted the pervasive connection between whiteness and Jesus. In any case, by the time their grandchild came along, Jesus was Black and could only be Black. Even the coloring book with a full-color picture of white Jesus on the cover—a gift that was placed into my young hands at church after I had given my Easter speech—somehow mysteriously disappeared between the time the gift was presented and the time we got home from church that same day.

I was an adult before I understood the gift my grandparents had given me: an image of God-in-flesh who looked like me, had hair like me, and had brown skin like mine. My grandparents never knew James Cone's *Black Theology and Black Power* or Albert Cleage's *The Black Messiah*; Black Jesus wasn't an academic or scholarly subject for them, as neither had finished high school. I imagine that this particular image of Jesus was born from the very depths of their faith and experience, an implicit rejection of a divine One who did not look like them. Black Jesus on our wall was an act of solidarity with marginalized people—all those who have had very few tools of resistance against dominant depictions of whiteness but who have a deep sense that God is on their side. And perhaps even more important than his skin tone was the fact that Black Jesus was a very present help in times of trouble, a close friend whose name was called in our house again and again.

As a child, I thought of Jesus as a very close neighbor, because calling on Jesus was like calling on Miss Priscilla next door—there was sure to be an immediate physical response. Miss Priscilla was the tenderhearted neighborhood busybody, perpetually clad in a floral housecoat, who lived to help others so that she could be first on the scene of any potential gossip. She could be at your door before you hung up the phone to invite her over, and she never failed to show up when called.

The Jesus of my grandmother's house was not just "Lord"; he was friend and confidant. Jesus came by to visit us on a regular basis, and for much of my early life, I thought that was just how it was everywhere that people believed. I thought everybody knew Jesus as a good neighbor who visited often. We called on Jesus when the groceries ran low or when someone's fever ran high. We called on Jesus when the rent check was due or when death visited and laid us low. And we called on Jesus in celebration and times of joy—when bodies were healed and prayers were answered and relationships were restored. Gospel artist John P. Kee's lyrics "Jesus is real, I know the Lord is real to me" perfectly describe the atmosphere of a home where Jesus visited often.

My grandmother's internal clock rang early, and so she rose early in the morning to pray. I learned, when older, to sleep through her morning libations, but as a little girl, I would often sneak out of bed to hear her talk to Jesus. She knelt down beside her bed to pray, and she taught me that kneeling was the proper form in which to pray. Even when saying grace while seated at the kitchen table, she somehow evoked a kneeling posture. "Every knee will bow" were the words on her lips when she kneeled along with me at night at the side of my tiny twin bed. It would be a long time and a long way away until I learned to pray without bending my body in half. Even now I sometimes wonder whether the reason Jesus doesn't seem to hear my prayers is that I no longer kneel.

My grandmother, who seemed so tall to my six-year-old self, would daily fold her body in half in order to sit at the feet of Jesus. Even when she was in her last years and pain was wracking her body, she would still kneel in respect and reverence while she waited for Jesus to "come on by here." She sang and prayed, and sometimes she moaned and hummed. But most often she just had conversations with her beloved friend—a friend who saw fit to intervene in her life on a regular basis. While she was in prayer, anyone else in the household, believer or skeptic, surely felt the presence of the divine. I would listen very quietly as she completely unburdened herself before Jesus in the way of two longtime friends who barely have to finish their sentences to make their thoughts known to each other. She would start to say something, and then she would start to sing, and then she would finish the thought with a hum. "For we know not what we should pray for as we ought," Paul writes in Romans 8:26, "but the Spirit itself maketh intercession for us with groanings which cannot be uttered."

And somewhere in there, I knew that this intimate conversation encompassed her prayer language, that this time with Jesus was her sweet hour of prayer.

❋ ❋ ❋

There is a haunting photo of Danella Bryant taken during the civil rights movement. An African American seventeen-year-old and Parker High School senior, Danella was among the many children and teens who were active in the movement in Alabama. During a demonstration outside the Traffic Engineering Building in Birmingham on May 5, 1963, a news photographer captured her praying. In the photograph she is kneeling on the concrete and grass, her hands clasped as tears stream down her face. Although they are outside the frame of this particular picture, other photos from that day show the water hoses and police dogs and armed law enforcement officials waiting to break up the demonstration—an unarmed group of children.

The picture evokes powerful emotions. Perhaps it's her youthfulness or the gloves in her hands or the look of pain in her eyes. And while kneel-ins and prayer vigils were a regular feature of the civil rights movement, this image of a singular, young Black teenager's body in prayer is particularly striking. The viewer is prompted to wonder what she is praying for at this particular moment. Is it a prayer for her safety and that of others? Is it a plea to end the violence being brutally inflicted upon nonviolent Black bodies? Is it a petition to simply make it home safely to her parents? And does God ultimately hear and answer her prayer?

This evocative image illustrates all the ways that prayer in the African American context is both deeply personal and highly communal. Danella Bryant is kneeling and crying; it is a scene of her own personal anguish. But just outside the frame of her own moment of prayer is an entire community of other Black teens and children—some also praying, some protesting, some shielding others from violence. Her prayer is not a moment of inaction. It is an active calling on the divine presence in the middle of a literal battle.

Black Christian churches of every denomination affirm the role of the "prayer warrior": a person committed to praying on behalf of others, someone willing to do spiritual battle against the powers, forces, and principalities that oppress. Encountering this photo as an adult reinforced the theology of prayer I learned as a child while kneeling at the foot of my grandmother's bed.

Prayer is a contradiction. One may feel profoundly alone in the moment of prayer, but when you enter before the throne of grace, the divine is present. And while the kneeling position—body bent, hands folded—may seem like a posture of submission, prayer itself can be a battle. The prayer warrior proclaims, along with Jacob in Genesis, who wrestles with God until daybreak, "I will not let go until you bless me." The prayer warrior can tarry for hours on behalf of herself and others. Prayer is that contradictory space where a powerless and defenseless mortal being dares to communicate with a powerful and omnipotent God. And prayer is where the imperfection of the human condition meets God's perfecting greatness. God is the Great Physician, the Great Lawmaker, and God's unsurpassed greatness stands above limited human capacity.

Prayer is a petition. It is a cry for help, a supplication, a plea for assistance. Prayer is the acknowledgment of weakness: that in our own strength and power, we are insufficient for the burdens we face. And yet there is a God capable of the miraculous. There is a God who answers prayer, sometimes with a yes and sometimes with a no. The supplicant can ask anything her heart desires; there is no petition too big or too small. And yet the act of prayer never absolves the petitioner from doing her part. You pray with your feet. At some point, you must leave your prayer closet with a plan of action and a resolve to make a change.

Prayer is intercession. It is the act of standing in the cosmic gap for others. There are those who cannot pray for themselves: those who are too weary and too sick, those who are too young or too old, and those who cannot or choose not to pray. Prayer is a reminder that somewhere, somebody is calling your name before God. The names of the sick and the shut-ins, which are carefully listed in church bulletins in Black churches across the nation, offer a small reminder that someone had you on their mind and took the time to pray for you.

Prayer is also celebration. It is gratitude for what God has done, large and small, known and unknown. You pray to celebrate waking up in the morning. You pray to celebrate a reasonable portion of health and strength. You pray to celebrate the food, clothing, and shelter you have—or even to give thanks that what you lack at the moment will eventually be provided. You pray to celebrate being protected from unseen dangers. You pray to celebrate those glimpses of God's goodness while you are yet in the land of the living.

Perhaps what I learned most clearly as a young child, kneeling in prayer with my grandmother, is that for the believer, prayer is a primary form of speech. I was the subject of many of my grandmother's prayers. The sacrifices of motherhood, yet again folded into grandmotherhood, were often more than she felt she could bear. But she felt it her duty to petition Jesus on my behalf. She prayed for me until I learned to pray for myself. And then she prayed for me some more.

"I am my ancestors' wildest dreams" is a poignant slogan within the African American community. Chattel slavery failed to crush the hopes and dreams of enslaved people. I do not know whether I have managed to achieve anything beyond which my hypothetical ancestors may have dreamed. But I am certain, without a shadow of a doubt, that my survival is a result of my grandmother's prayers. She prayed for me with an intensity, fervor, and sense of obligation that no one has ever matched. She prayed degrees and graduations and career accomplishments into existence—answers to prayer she would not live to see. As we knelt at the foot of my childhood bed, my grandmother introduced me to Jesus. She did not introduce me to religion. She gave me Jesus.

Outside of church, I never heard much about God the Father. For my grandmother, Jesus was the lover of her soul. Jesus was the burden bearer. Jesus was the heart fixer and the mind regulator. Jesus was the subject of her songs when she baked biscuits on Sunday morning. Jesus was the love on her lips when she pressed my hair in the kitchen on Saturday night. Jesus would show up when my grandmother had coffee with Mother Johnson. Jesus would stop by when the missionary circle met in our house. The six-year-old me would not have hesitated to run and borrow a cup of sugar or two cups of flour from our neighbor Jesus, like I would from Ms. Tina down the hall, because that is how real he was to my grandmother. My grandmother called on the name of Jesus because for her, there was power just in the name.

※ ※ ※

Reverend Dr. Anna Pauline Murray (1910–1985) was a poet, lawyer, feminist, and priest. Born in Baltimore, Maryland,

Murray, known as Pauli, became the first Black woman ordained as an Episcopal priest in 1977 at the age of sixty-seven. She was an activist for civil rights and women's rights from the 1940s through the 1970s. She spent much of her career as a lawyer, legal scholar, policy analyst, and teacher. She held faculty appointments at Benedict College and Brandeis University. The NAACP used her work during the *Brown v. Board of Education* desegregation case in 1954, and much of her legal work laid the foundation for the current field of feminist jurisprudence. A cofounder of the National Organization for Women, Murray coined the term *Jane Crow* to articulate the ways that the racist Jim Crow laws specifically affected African American women.

In 1963, she became one of the first to criticize the sexism of the civil rights movement, particularly in her speech "The Negro Woman and the Quest for Equality." In that speech, among other grievances, she criticized the fact that in the 1963 March on Washington, no women were invited to make any of the major speeches. No women were invited to be part of the march's delegation of leaders who went to the White House. Murray eventually resigned her tenured professorship at Brandeis University to enter seminary. After her ordination, she offered the Eucharist for the first time at the Chapel Hill church where her grandmother had been baptized as a slave. She worked as a parish priest in Washington, DC, until her death in 1985.

Throughout her long legal and political career and her brief ministry, Murray wrote poetry, with her earliest dated poem from 1933. Much of it is about faith. Having walked away from the church for a significant period, she returned with a deep sense of calling to the priesthood. Her poems draw upon liturgical elements from the Episcopal tradition, particularly the Book of Common Prayer, as well as her lifetime of experiences as a Black queer woman living through legal segregation.

When I first encountered the work and life of Pauli Murray, I initially thought about how different the world she occupied was from the one in which my grandmother lived. Murray was formally educated with several degrees (Hunter College, Howard University, Yale University); she was raised in the high church tradition of the Episcopal Church; she was queer, gender non-conforming, and perhaps transgender; and she was an occupant of weighty political and civic worlds, with friends including Eleanor Roosevelt, Ruth Bader Ginsburg, and Martin Luther King Jr.

It was only in Murray's poetry that I heard echoes of what she and my grandmother shared. They were both granddaughters of enslaved persons who deeply loved the name of Jesus.

In her poem "Nazarene," Murray offers no Christian apologetic, no defense of the divinity of Jesus of Nazareth. She offers no theological treatise on whether the Jesus of history is the same Christ of faith. Some say, she writes, that Jesus is just a "legend" or "hippy poet." Others, she continues, argue that Jesus is merely the dream of "slaves and beggars," Karl Marx's "opium of the people." Murray refuses to even affirm certain orthodox Christian beliefs, such as the doctrine that Jesus performed miracles and had a teaching ministry. The only thing her poem insists upon is that the name of Jesus has power. To call on Jesus, Murray suggests, is to evoke a name that embodies sacrificial love: "that gift of pain / That only love can bear / And having borne still cry / I love."

Two Black women—each barely two generations removed from slavery, with radically different upbringings and trajectories—call upon a name that means to them the pain of sacrifice as well as the radical hope of love. This is the heart of womanist theology: the needs of real human people before doctrine.

For whom and for what causes are we willing to sacrifice? How do we demonstrate that we love ourselves and our neighbors? Will we love ourselves enough to insist on our inalienable rights, kneeling in the face of water hoses and police dogs? The Episcopalian Howard- and Yale-educated lawyer, the Pentecostal domestic worker: these women may have formally belonged to two different denominations with vastly different theologies. But to both of them, as Black women navigating a cruel and indifferent world, the name of Jesus meant hope, and life, and strength.

As a womanist, I understand Jesus not through a study of Mary, Joseph, and the birth of the Christ child. My Christology begins at the foot of my bed, with a grandmother teaching me to sing words I have hidden in my heart and to which I return even when my prayers sometimes fail. These words, first penned as a poem by Frederick Whitfield in 1861 and later set to music, never fail to remind me of a grandmother calling on Jesus, with a certainty and intimacy I may never know:

> *There is a name I love to hear,*
> *I love to sing its worth;*
> *It sounds like music in mine ear,*
> *The sweetest name on earth.*

2 Just above My Head

"Your love is too thick," he said. . . . "Too thick?" she said. . . .
"Love is or it ain't. Thin love ain't love at all."

—TONI MORRISON, *BELOVED*

Before we walk into the sanctuary, Mother Johnson hands me a lace doily to cover my head. When Mother Johnson gives me the head covering, she does not speak; her simple gesture is enough for me to obey. My arms immediately adjust the small comb attached to the head covering within my twists. There is no need to look into a mirror, because although it has been at least twenty years since I have done this, I know by mere touch that my covering is properly placed. Even the hairs on my head seem to fall back into a habit from so long ago.

I know I do not have to wear the head covering Mother Johnson has offered me. As a guest, no longer a member of this congregation, I could decline, and no one would expect me to do otherwise. At a glance, I see that pretty much no woman under the age of seventy covers her head. Everyone knows Mother Johnson is a traditionalist, a holdout when it comes to older customs, and most people now ignore the traditions she keeps. To me, she is an ancient and ageless woman who was already old when I was young. Yet the twenty years that have passed since I saw her last have not diminished her spirit.

Church mothers like Mother Johnson are a formidable force. These older Black women are the power brokers in many African American congregations. Even in a hierarchical structure with male bishops and pastors, church mothers wield authority like they wield their tambourines. In some denominations, the "church mother" is an ecclesial office, with a specified set of duties and obligations, particularly to train younger women in the faith. Even in denominations without officially appointed church mothers, there is a cadre of older Black women whose wisdom, experience, and longevity within the congregation give them a position of respect and authority.

The feeling of the lace doily is barely discernible, and yet the weight of years of memories presses down on me. With that featherweight material on my head, we enter the sanctuary together, with Mother Johnson quietly reminding me that "holiness is right."

Holiness is right: it was a catchall phrase meant to remind us that as Christians, particularly as Pentecostals, we were to live in the world but not be of the world. It was the phrase repeated when someone's skirt was too short or someone's head was uncovered in the sanctuary. It was the phrase that barred drinking alcohol and going to the movies. It was the phrase that condemned lipstick and nail polish. Holiness is right: it attempted to impose a legalistic definition of what it meant to be a faithful witness for Christ. It led to a list composed mainly of "thou shalt nots."

The Holiness-Pentecostal Church is an entire branch of American Christianity that developed in the nineteenth and twentieth centuries in the United States. Its churches place an emphasis on what is called the "baptism of the Holy Spirit," sanctification from sin, and a life of holiness. The early Holiness-Pentecostal movement urged followers to live by a strict moral code. The modern Pentecostal church rose out of the Holiness movement and can be traced back to Los Angeles and the Azusa Street Revival of 1906: a series of worship services in which largely poor people of color sought a deeper experience of the Holy Spirit.

My longing for holiness was birthed on the hard benches of all-night tarry services like the ones the people of Azusa Street attended. Tarry services lasted from evening until the next morning as the believers shut themselves in the sanctuary to pray, sing, worship, and tarry through the entire night in expectation of God doing miraculous things. But those services also gave rise to a deep skepticism about legalism masquerading as holiness. I struggled with the tension between the unending lists and shifting terrain of codes of conduct, on the one hand, and my developing realization that holiness has everything to do with the state of my heart, on the other.

Holiness is right was also the phrase that created a longing in my soul for genuine holiness: not a code of conduct dependent on rigid interpretation of doctrine but the fear and awe and wonder of living a life that is pleasing and acceptable to a holy God. My quest for a life of holiness has not removed me from the cares and complications of this world. In fact, holiness requires an active and present concern and engagement in the gritty reality of a fallen world. Of what purpose is a holy life if it is hidden out of fear of entanglement with the messiness around you? If we are so holy that we are afraid to walk outside our doors lest temptation beset us, then our holiness has no power and no purpose. Genuine holiness is a beacon of love; it is a light engaging the world.

Holiness is not a perfect life but a life lived with intentionality and purpose. It is holy to love others, even when you do not understand them. It is holy to sow goodness, even when you are constantly confronted with evil. It is holy to work for justice, even when the case for justice has long been denied.

Holiness is a longing for God. When we seek God with our whole hearts and our whole beings, we know holiness. When we surrender our worries to God with the knowledge that even the grains of sand on the beach are numbered, we know holiness. When we rejoice in God's faithfulness and when we lament God's silence, we know holiness.

Holiness demands neither a dress code nor a list of rules. The open Communion table is holy because all, regardless of status, creed, or color, are welcomed. The spontaneous fellowship that happens when two or three saints gather is holy, because no formal program is needed to worship God. The laughter and joy of a full dinner table are holy, because we are called to nourish both body and spirit.

Holiness draws us closer to God, to each other, and to our innermost selves. Holiness requires grace, not the shackles of legalism. To be holy as God is holy is to imitate the love of God in all that we do. I was the product of people who loved me, loved God, and firmly believed that if you raised a child in the church, they would never depart from it. And in that respect, the community of this tiny Holiness church in Brooklyn entirely succeeded.

Growing up, I felt Mother Johnson unfairly singled me out for attention. Among all the church mothers, she was the one with the biggest list of "thou shall nots," the most vocal when young women appeared to violate any of the unwritten rules. When I was a teenager, she constantly admonished me for wearing pants in the sanctuary. When I explained that I was arriving at a Tuesday- or Friday-night service straight from volleyball practice, she would insist I change into a skirt in the bathroom. She was the one who noticed the clear lip gloss I dared to wear at fourteen and forced me to wipe it off. My own grandmother did not monitor me as closely for infractions as she did. Mother Johnson caught every skirt that was a millimeter too short; every hint that I was talking to a boy in the congregation; every rumor that I had gone to a movie or failed to dutifully arrive at service multiple times a week. She called all of this holiness that befits a child of God. The older I got and the more I read, the only things I could call this constant monitoring of my body were oppressive and patriarchal.

Reading will change you. In his first autobiography, written in 1845, Frederick Douglass maintains that the primary opposition to teaching enslaved people to read was that it would "forever unfit them" to be enslaved. That is how I felt when I first arrived at college and began reading work written by feminists. I began to understand how the monitoring of clothing and behavior was a form of social control, growing mostly out of fear that women would become "unruly" and step out of their place. I learned how patriarchal cultures, particularly religious ones, sought to stifle women's voices, agency, and power. I read through two thousand years of Christian history and could see the patterns repeat themselves: a literalist reading of Christian scripture ("Women, be silent") combined with man-made traditions always led to restrictions on women's ordination, women's participation in certain sacraments, women's leadership roles, and even women's theological work. I thought about all the churches I had encountered in my youth, in which women were allowed to speak from the floor but not from the pulpit, or in which women could "teach" and "exhort" and "testify" but could not preach. College gave me a vocabulary, words such as *patriarchy* and *hegemony* and *dominance*, to describe so much of what I had seen in church as a child. And those cultural norms and traditions were most often maintained by women.

Reading, once I got to college, gave me the words to express something I had always seen and felt but did not have the language to describe: patriarchy is a structure that requires the participation of both men and women to uphold it. In all my growing-up years in the Holiness tradition, no men had ever commented on the length of my skirt or my uncovered head. They did not have to say a word with women so eager to police and enforce these arbitrary standards.

Reading will change you, and reading in context will change you even more. It was not until graduate school that I encountered texts that not only helped me to understand the patriarchy of American Christianity but that put that information into conversation with the African American context. Reading Delores Williams, the first womanist theologian I ever encountered, was like encountering manna from heaven. In her book *Sisters in the Wilderness: The Challenge of Womanist God-Talk*, she centers Black women's experiences, taking seriously the lives of Black church women like Mother Johnson and my grandmother and the generations of church women who raised me.

For example, while maintaining that the sins of sexism and patriarchy infect the American church, including African American churches, Williams also offers this poignant observation: "Reflection upon black women's sources revealed to me the survival strategies they have used to keep the community alive and hopeful. The strategies I saw were: 1) an art of cunning; 2) an art of encounter; 3) an art of care; and 4) an art of connecting. I use the word *act* here to indicate the high level of skill many black women developed as they created and adapted strategies to ensure their survival and that of their families."

Williams argues that if we dare to take seriously the context in which Black women live and move, we will understand their theology. When I read about the art of cunning, which

Williams describes as "knowledge combined with manual skill and dexterity," I began to wonder whether there was more to the legalism in which I had been raised than first appeared. Could this legalism be less a simplistic and restrictive reading of scriptures the church mothers loved to quote at me and more a survival strategy?

I had spent most of my life under the assumption that these Black church women were engaged in simple hermeneutics—specifically, a literalist reading of the biblical text. Mother Johnson would quote 1 Corinthians 11:5, reminding me that "every woman that prayeth or prophesieth with her head uncovered dishonoureth her head." There were countless Bible study lessons about the Proverbs 31 woman: her modesty, her usefulness, her prioritizing of care for the family. We were drilled in scriptures about the wages of sin, lest we stumble and backslide. But reading Delores Williams helped me to understand that Black women are also pulling theological source material from their own lives and not just from the Christian scripture. How they understand God and holiness and modesty is rooted both in the Word and in the world.

I started paying attention to that source material. I started paying attention to the stories of the women raising me at home and in the church. I started reading history that centered Black women's lived experiences. And I discovered facts that challenged my simplistic understanding of their theologies. These women had worked in other people's kitchens, homes, and laundromats to provide for their families. They had toiled in fields and in factories. And through it all, they faced sexual abuse, accusations of hypersexuality, and other forms of sexual trauma. And whether in their workplaces or in their own homes, Black women's bodies were the constant subject of scrutiny. Hips and breasts and hair and bottoms were the subject of unwelcome touches, jokes, "evidence" of sexual prowess, and surveillance. And for some women in the Black church, modest dressing and legalistic codes became necessary for their very survival. Modesty was their attempt to displace unwanted attention from eyes that reduced them to their sexual function and that stripped from them the fullness of their humanity.

I realized that I had been raised by women busily focused on my survival and their own. They wielded the scripture as their defense against a world in which Black women were devalued and defined by their bodies. They were trying to keep me safe from predators both in the church and outside of it. They were trying to keep me busy with tasks and responsibilities at church and in the home because they wanted me to survive. Knowing that I only had a short time under their influence, and knowing that college and life would pull me away from their teaching, these church mothers spent sixteen years instilling virtues of modesty and holiness within me. The modest clothing, the head covering I was forced to wear as a teenager that marked me as a child of the church—these screamed "Stay away!" to the teenaged boys at the corner. Even if these boys could not have articulated it, they knew from my appearance that I was a "marked" daughter of the church and that someone was looking out for me. They knew someone loved me and would fight for me.

I was raised by church mothers who could not have protected themselves against rape in the fields of sharecroppers or assault in the offices of white men. I was raised by women who feared police intervention in their own homes and therefore had no means of defense against predatory fathers and brothers and uncles. And so they taught me to deflect attention away from my body in hopes that I would be left alone and allowed to grow up undisturbed. They did what they knew to do, using the coping strategies their own mothers and grandmothers had taught them. Even as they chastised me for the length of my skirts, they prayed a hedge of protection around me and anointed me with oil.

These church mothers vocalized only one part of the message to the group of girls growing up under their watch: Cover yourself. But returning to that Holiness church as an adult, I could hear the whole message, the words that went unvoiced by Mother Johnson and the others: Cover yourself, because this world eats up little Black girls, and I want to spare you from some of the pain I know all too well.

I did not know then, and I do not know now, Mother Johnson's personal story. In the narcissism of adolescence, I never bothered to ask her about her own life. I am now left grappling with only the few facts I can recall, including the startling remembrance that she had no husband or children of her own in a congregation filled with families. Like my own grandmother, she was Southern born and a refugee who fled Jim and Jane Crow. I'll never know what drove her to take on me and other girls in the church as her special projects. I can only sit with the knowledge that the road could not have been easy for her. In a world that has no love for impoverished Black women, she had survived, and she was trying to pass on some of her survival skills to us.

I spent years resenting a theology that seemed so overbearing and shaming, a theology rooted in hiding the body and crucifying the flesh. But the very fact of my survival—of my thriving—is connected to the love, care, and wisdom of women who knew harsh truths about the world they wanted to spare me from learning firsthand.

Black women are made in the likeness of God—in the *imago dei*. This is not a radical concept. So why would we not draw from the source material of their lives for theological reflection?

Why does the field of theology continue to elevate the lives and teachings of white men as somehow the "standard" approach for understanding doctrine or theology, accusing Black women or Asian women or other theologians of color of merely writing from their particular contexts? All theology is contextual, because it emerges from the lived realities of those who are writing, reflecting, and creating language for understanding who God is. No one can attempt to know and understand the divine without tapping into their very human, very concrete experience.

Womanist theology, with its explicit concern about the lives of Black women, speaks for those who make up two-thirds or more of the laity in the Black church, in which the leadership is unquestionably male. It is critical that Black women share, write, and process their own stories and those of their forebearers and ancestors. Otherwise, when others attempt to explain their stories, usually relying upon unfounded stereotypes, a certain violence is reenacted upon Black women's lives.

The story of Margaret Garner, an enslaved woman who killed her own daughter, distills the atrocities of American slavery. As a student at an Ivy League university, I sat in a classroom and learned about the real-life story of the woman upon whom African American novelist Toni Morrison based her novel *Beloved*. Garner was likely the product of rape and the daughter of her owner; many enslaved Black women were subjected to systematic sexual abuse by slaveholders, and some gave birth to children who were siblings of their white masters' children. Sold to her first owner's younger brother, who likely raped her and also fathered some of her children, Margaret Garner was married to an enslaved man, Robert Garner. In 1856, as a family, they attempted an escape from slavery. While they were on the run and in the process of being captured by US marshals, the mother killed her youngest daughter, who was two years old, rather than allow her to face reenslavement. Garner was jailed and tried for this killing, which generated significant media coverage in both Northern and Southern newspapers. There was national outrage among proslavery advocates. How dare an enslaved woman, herself legal property, kill her child, who was deemed the property of someone else? Under the auspices of slavery, Garner's children were not her own.

Concerning this case, white abolitionist Lucy Stone writes in Garner's defense, "The faded faces of the Negro children tell too plainly to what degradation the female slaves submit. Rather than give her daughter to that life, she killed it. If in her deep maternal love she felt the impulse to send her child back to God, to save it from coming woe, who shall say she had no right not to do so?"

I sat in that classroom, navigating primary documents of the Garner case, with fear and trembling. The horror of rape. The death of a child. The fear of a return to bondage. The utter impossibility of hope. I am not sure whether I have cried in a classroom since that time, but I remember choking back tears while trying to maintain an intellectual façade about a woman who could be one of my own ancestors. *Beloved*, a fictionalized account of the story, is a powerful work of beauty. Morrison takes the reader from the Middle Passage of the eighteenth century to the institutionalized system of enslavement of the nineteenth century. She weaves together a love story of an enslaved couple with the ghost story of a dead child. Yet reading the unadulterated facts of what Margaret Garner endured, and others whose names we do not know, grieved my spirit. How could my ancestors have endured so much and survived? How could this mother have sacrificed so much? How much more can Black women endure from this cruel world?

One of my classmates in that seminar room was a young white man whom I had gotten to know as part of a Christian fellowship on campus. We shared the same vocabulary, as we were both kids who had grown up in church. We brought those teachings, that language, and those values to school with us. Our shared Christian background seemed to close the gap between our very different circumstances: me, a young Black woman, first-generation college student, with the legacy of generations of poverty; and he, a young white man, from a family of privilege and affluence, with a family legacy at this institution.

That day I sat and listened as this young man first publicly identified himself as a Christian and then insisted that, according to his principles, it was unimaginable and immoral that a mother would kill her child, no matter the circumstances. He argued that since Garner had claimed to be a Christian, she should have trusted God and submitted herself to the authorities when she and her family were captured. She should have returned to slavery without resistance, and then she, her children, and her husband would have been "safe."

Sometimes small moments change you so profoundly that you walk away a different person. This was such a moment for me. I suddenly knew without a doubt that the God I believed in and served was not the same God in whom my classmate believed. His God required a return to enslavement and submission to death. He believed that safety was possible under the yoke of bondage, and he valued obedience over freedom. Before I had the vocabulary that liberation theology would later give me, everything within me refuted the claims of my classmate. I believe that Garner resisted the yoke of slavery with every fiber of her being and that her resistance was an act of faith. I believe that a life under bondage was already a form of death, and she believed in a liberating God who could deliver her from the hell she faced on earth.

I thought about the horrors Black women endured, many of which I was reading about in this classroom for the first time. I thought about their historical and contemporary strategies for survival, the likes of which my own grandmother and church mothers had to employ. And I could only come to one conclusion: sometimes death may be better than life. Garner killed her child as an act of mercy. Enslaved people sometimes chose the sweetness of death over the bitterness of chattel slavery.

My classmate and I argued in that seminar room. Although we would spend more years together on the same campus, that was the last time we would speak to each other. I could no longer attend a Christian fellowship where he and others shared similar views. Any God who would insist a mother return her child to slavery, to be brutalized, raped, sold, or worse—all for the sake of godly obedience and submission—was far too hateful a God for me to serve.

The historical source material to which I was being exposed made my theology more complicated but much stronger. The words of James Baldwin came closest to my liberatory theology that was emerging from these college classrooms: "If the concept of God has any validity or any use, it can only be to make us larger, freer, and more loving. If God cannot do this, then it is time we got rid of Him." Since I could never get rid of the God I learned at my grandmother's knee, I began to embrace the concept of a larger, freer, and more loving God.

Sometimes I think about my ancestors who jumped off slave ships and drowned themselves in the ocean. I think about my ancestors who hid in maroon communities, living off the land in defiance of slave codes. I think about my ancestors who smothered children before the auction block separated nursing infants from mothers. I think about my ancestors who staged armed rebellions. And I know that they are among the great cloud of witnesses just above my head, urging me toward a faith that is holy and full of grace and also rooted and grounded in justice.

3   The Work of Her Hands

Now you all, prop me up on every leaning side. Don't let my hands fall. We're holding up the world with these hands.
—Zora Neale Hurston, *Moses, Man of the Mountain*

My grandmother's hands feel leathery. They are never soft or smooth. No amount of lotion can unharden the skin after years spent cleaning, scrubbing, cooking. Hands immersed in dirty water, clean water, harsh chemicals—hands that, combined with elbow grease, shined floors and windows and baseboards in white women's kitchens. Hands of an older, Southern Black woman . . . hands that quietly built a nation but whose history is often unrecorded. I have no memory of manicured hands holding mine. Instead, when I remember her hands, I can still feel the calluses of someone who only knew labor her whole life.

It is only now that I am much older that I can piece together the work of her hands. Strong young hands cutting tobacco in Southern fields; brown hands cradling the one long-desired child she dared to love after so many losses; tentative hands signing legal documents she did not understand for a new life up North; gentle hands walking her abandoned granddaughter to school. My grandmother's hands are a love story, but they are not smooth, not soft, not easy. No real love story is. Her hands are a love story of survival in hard places, during hard times.

These hands parted small sections of hair, oiled a dry scalp, and made neat piles of shiny braids. These same hands, which had scrubbed toilets and diapered other women's babies, would take the smallest of barrettes or beads or balls and place them securely at the end of tiny plaits, in alternating patterns and colors, securing them at the ends with tiny rubber bands. The creativity of brown hands, denied an artist's palette, found joy in arranging the colorful beads of her granddaughter's hair. These hands, which had never touched a potter's wheel or blank canvas, created beauty from braids. Rough, callused, heavy hands loved my tender young scalp. These hands, so large to my child's eyes, threaded an impossibly tiny needle, and from fabric scraps they made dolls and quilts and magic. I would later have no trouble believing in the *creatio ex nihilo*—the idea that God created the cosmos out of nothing—because all my life I had watched my grandmother prepare a feast from an empty refrigerator and bare cabinets. She taught me that to be a Black woman in this world is to learn how to make something from nothing.

Sometimes I look at my professionally manicured hands and feel a sting of hot shame. Shame at not being able to fully comprehend the generational sacrifices made on my behalf. Shame for ever having been embarrassed to wear Easter dresses sewn by those hands when my friends wore fancier ones purchased at Macy's. Shame for once rejecting the food those hands cooked in favor of something at the local fast-food place. And shame when I wonder whether my hands will ever produce something that leaves so enduring a legacy.

There could well have been a sign above the door of my childhood home reading, "Idle hands are the devil's workshop." Idleness was as offensive as disobedience or lying; all were sins for which you would be swiftly punished. But idleness in children seemed to be a particular offense that the adults in my life could scarcely tolerate. The idea that a child would have nothing to do, would not be productive in some way, was unthinkable. This led to a childhood of cooking, cleaning, sweeping, dusting, and running errands. No one was going to sit in my grandmother's house and be lazy. She woke me up early on Saturday mornings, the one day of the week I could have conceivably slept a bit later, with a list of things that needed to be done. Saturday merely existed to prepare us for the hours we would spend in church on Sunday.

I spent hours—days and weeks and years—in my grandmother's kitchen, helping her cook. Cooking was a full-contact sport. It first required a spotless kitchen, and a kitchen was not spotless if there was so much as one dirty spoon in the sink. After what seemed like hours just preparing the space, you had to be willing to get your hands dirty if you wanted to cook. There were no recipes in my grandmother's kitchen, no notecards with lists of ingredients. Each dish we prepared had a little bit of this, a dash of that, with a little more of this over here. I learned to roll dough for peach cobbler and make perfect circles for buttermilk biscuits. I had to experiment until the crust for sweet-potato pie was acceptable to discerning adult palates. I worked at seasonings until I could produce a batch of collard greens worthy of approval. I learned to cook by cooking, rolling up my sleeves, getting my hands dirty, making mistakes, starting over, cleaning up, tasting along the way, and doing it again week after week.

A child learning to cook quickly learns the kitchen can be a dangerous place for young hands. Chopping and grating, hot oil and hot ovens, constant cleaning and scrubbing left my hands raw. One day, as a teenager with far too much attitude, I dared to suggest that a food processor could do almost all the things we did by hand—tasks that were incredibly labor-intensive and time-consuming. My grandmother looked curiously at me and my suggestion for a moment, and then she went right back to singing and chopping without so much as a response. I knew better than to ask again.

Cooking was her ministry, and I witnessed as she ministered to the lonely and the sick and the lost with a Bible in one hand and a freshly baked pound cake in the other. She fed everyone who came within a fifty-foot radius of our door, always greeting people with both food and scripture. She told me that Jesus consistently did three things: healed people, told stories, and fed people. And that is all she, as a follower of Jesus, had to do in order to live a life pleasing to God. The food from my grandmother's kitchen healed people, not because of the ingredients but because the person who prepared that food was never afraid to sit with the sick and dying. She was never too busy or too tired to feed welcome guests and strangers.

Years later, in that same kitchen while performing the same set of chores, my grandmother, unprompted, responded to my suggestion as if no time had passed: "You don't need a food processor. You've got to know how to cook a meal for an entire family with your bare hands and one good knife." I have no idea what prompted a return to the idea I had brought up years ago and had long forgotten. I learned that the pearls of wisdom from my grandmother emerged at the strangest times and places. She did not elaborate on her pronouncement, and we simply continued our well-practiced kitchen routine.

Her words, however, stirred a prophetic question: When there is no outside help, can you still perform the task to which you have been assigned? When you have a few scraps—food, fabric, money, strength—can your hands make them into something more?

Despite my current kitchen being filled with gadgets, I still enjoy the process of getting my hands messy, kneading dough or grating cheese, and knowing the work of my own hands is sufficient to produce a simple meal or an elaborate feast.

❀ ❀ ❀

We sang all the verses of every hymn at church. And while it may have been the chorus that was given two, three, even four rounds of congregational singing, the words of the verses still somehow managed to seep deep into our spirits. And just like everyone had a favorite passage of scripture, everyone had a favorite verse from an old hymn. Thomas Dorsey's "Precious Lord, Take My Hand" was the hymn that echoed in my childhood home. With little skill but much enthusiasm, my grandmother would play the piano while she sang her favorite verse about the Lord taking her hand and leading her home.

"Precious Lord" is a hymn that leaves an impression on you. It is slow, melodic, haunting, and elegiac. It is a song of funerals and sorrow and grief. And because I heard this particular verse so much, I had to wrestle with the sublime beauty of the phrase "lest I fall." That was the terror that haunted any good Holy Ghost–filled Christian: to fall away from faith, to fall out of love with God.

As I grew older, my faith matured, shifted, and changed, becoming something that would be barely recognizable to the tradition into which I was born. That shift left me to wonder at times whether I had fallen away from my childhood faith— whether I had fallen out of love with my grandmother's God. The doctrine and dogma I had been taught did not make any sense to me anymore. The legalistic practices I had been raised to obey seemed completely contradictory and hypocritical. I feared the exact thing the saints had warned me about when they sent me off to college had come to fruition: I had gotten some "learning" and forgotten the "burning" of a holy and righteous God.

It wasn't that I stopped believing. I believed, always, in Something, Someone, some loving hands that had set my very existence into motion. I believed even in those moments in which God's presence was so distant and so dim that the hymns of my childhood could barely penetrate my heart. But the childhood faith had to fall away so that an adult faith could be born.

I let go of a wrathful God, a God lurking around every corner and waiting to punish me for any infraction, and began to embrace a loving God who looked beyond my faults and saw my needs. I let go of deeply embedded homophobia and xenophobia and patriarchy, biases that had been unconsciously transmitted to me all my life, and began to embrace a generous, affirming, and liberatory faith. I let go of the denials of all pleasure, the castigation of the body, the rebuke of the frivolous and silly, and began to embrace the joys of simple pleasures and healthy satisfactions. I let go of the arrogant confidence that had been instilled in me—that what I had been taught was the only right, true, and holy way, and that there was no other path—and began to embrace the most important theological posture that any believer can have: God is beyond my comprehension, and waiting on God is simply the best I can do.

While waiting on my Precious Lord, I discovered my own grown woman's hands. Hands that were stronger than I imagined they could be; hands that were more capable than I imagined they could be; hands that both clenched into fists and relaxed into prayers. I discovered that the anger and the doubt and the unbelief that I had pushed as far down as they could go, like I had always been taught to do, were actually necessary for a mature faith to live. The hands I offered to God in prayer were those of an adult, making a choice on her own to find comfort in the companionship of a loving Friend.

I am a New Yorker, and we walk fast even when we have nowhere to go. So when I come up behind the young couple walking slowly and holding hands, taking up the entire sidewalk, I am frustrated. The sidewalk is narrow, and I am angrily walking behind them. The sidewalk is narrow, and I cannot pass them unless I walk into the busy street. I just want to get home, and I have no patience for their love, for their whispered words, for their entwined hands forming an obstacle between me and the clear path ahead. Exasperated by their pace, I am forced to slow my stride. In my impatience, I resolve to simply walk behind them until we can get to the curb, where I will overtake them at the light and give them a mean stare. They must be tourists, I think, the worst kind of tourists for this busy city sidewalk—young, clueless about their surroundings, and deeply in love.

I prepare my face to reflect my exasperation, and at the corner I turn to look at them and get ready to sigh audibly. I need them to see my face and hear how they have inconvenienced a whole city with their hand-holding human barrier. But what I see, when I truly look at them, startles me and convicts me. They are young, impossibly young, and so deeply in love that they cannot even register my face giving them my "fed up with slow-moving tourists" look. They are alone in this crowded city, cocooned in a place that my impatience and my ill temper cannot touch. He lifts her hand to his lips and kisses her fingers. I turn away, ashamed of my mean thoughts and embarrassed at witnessing such a deeply personal moment.

The set of tightly knit hands—that barricade against my efficient walking—is actually a protective hedge around this young love, a love that will be assailed on every side by forces small and great. Newly planted love needs encouragement and not angry glares of exasperation. I fix my face to offer them a smile and continue ahead of them. It occurs to me as I walk away that I am now rooting for them. I am now hoping that in fifty years, there will still be gentle kisses of hands lined with spots and wrinkles. I am praying that in twenty years, others will be able to witness their mature love, the love that stands the test of time. And though they are strangers to me, I want their loving cocoon to survive. I want them to succeed where so many of us have failed. I want for them an enduring love that weathers the storms and the sorrows that will surely head their way.

I needed this reminder: that most of the lessons I have learned about God's love have not come from inside the walls of the church. There were no Bible studies or Sunday-school lessons on how to fall in love or what to do when love breaks your heart. The tenderness between this young couple—their public displays of affection and their unapologetic love for each other—is a needed reminder that I am also worthy of gentle, compassionate, and unconditional love. They are a reminder that God intends for us to be in relationship with one another, that God has, in fact, created us for one another. They are a reminder that my midnight hour, or any season of loneliness, only lasts for a while and that joy does come in the morning.

There are seasons of loneliness for which the only remedy is to take your cares and concerns to the Lord in prayer. My grandmother called it the midnight hour, a season in which nothing can help but time spent with hands clasped in prayer and knees bent in supplication. A midnight hour can be any time of day, but it is a moment in which all your doubts, fears, and anxieties converge, leaving you feeling lost and alone. A midnight hour is when you regret the path you have taken or the job you have chosen. A midnight hour is when, despite having hundreds of names in your mobile contact list, you have no one who can understand the depth of your pain. A midnight hour is when God is silent or deaf or indifferent to your cries and pleas. A midnight hour is when you feel the weight of deep soul loneliness, whether there are people around or not.

We are reluctant to talk about the midnight hours in our lives. Perhaps it's the vulnerability of actually admitting our pain or our fear or our regret that stops us. We are invested in all the façades we have created, those in which we are happy, joyful, productive, never lonely, never scared, never vulnerable. We want to convince ourselves and others that we have it all together. But every once in a while, a midnight hour comes along that reveals our pretense—our failure to admit that there are still nights we cry ourselves to sleep; that there are still confrontations we are too scared to have; that there are still intimidating bullies on the adult playground; that there is still hurt and shame from wounds inflicted long ago. During my own season of loneliness, my own midnight hour, I found myself walking in lament on a busy city sidewalk.

The young couple, walking with intertwined hands, was my reminder that love, in all its wondrous forms, is a gift. And that the loving hands of a grandmother braiding hair, the burn-scarred hands of someone baking pies, and the tender hands of one's beloved are all God's beautiful work.

4 Leaving

And whosoever shall not receive you, nor hear your words,
when ye depart out of that house or city, shake off the dust of
your feet.

—Jesus, Matthew 10:14

It was a perfect night if you enjoy a good snowstorm. It was the
kind of snowstorm predicted well in advance, with classes preemptively canceled for the following day. And while students of
every age delight in the news of a snow day, teachers and professors rejoice even more, savoring a few additional hours to prepare
for the work ahead. Without an early-morning class to teach, I
was wide awake and transfixed by the beauty of this snowy night,
which I was enjoying from the comfort and warmth of my bed.

That peace was shattered when I heard the transformer blow. I watched out my window in awe at the shower of sparks it produced. Very quickly, the transformer pole caught on fire, burning dangerously close to the second-story bedroom in my 120-year-old house.

I made the 911 call; because this was a wealthy enclave in a small town, I could hear fire trucks in the distance before I had even given the dispatcher all the information about the incident. Borrowed privilege buys an immediate response to a frantic phone call at two o'clock on a Monday morning. The firefighters pulled up outside my house and immediately went to work, carefully navigating the heavy snow, which already seemed about two feet deep. I watched all this unfold like a dream until a very real knock on the door shattered my complacency. Fire personnel stood at the threshold, informing me that if they were not able to contain the situation, my daughter and I might need to evacuate. We'd have about five minutes.

What decisions do you need to make in the five minutes before you leave home in the middle of the night? Fearing the worst, and uncertain when you'll return, what do you take with you? What do you leave behind?

As I stood at the doorway in flannel pajamas and a robe, a certain peace washed over me. Maybe that was the first time I actually experienced a peace that passes all understanding—a peace that makes absolutely no sense given the circumstances.

As much as I loved this old house and every single object in it, it was easy to decide what to take and what to leave. There were no frantic movements during this five-minute window. No sitcom-style running between rooms and emptying out drawers. Somehow, during my grown-up Black woman years, I had learned how to deliberately and calmly leave a place.

The second knock of fire personnel revealed a family of two ready to face an uncertain future. I had awakened my tiny daughter and dressed her for the snowy weather outside, snow-suit and boots over her footie pajamas. She stood, so sleepy, at the bottom of the stairs with me, one hand in mine and the other clutching the one stuffed animal that was to be saved. Her collection was out of control, dozens of mementos of our travels and gifts from generous friends and family members. But there was a very special bear in her hands: the one that always got to sleep in her bed; the one that was very gently washed on the delicate cycle; the one that I had bought her before I even knew of her existence.

That same bear my three-year-old was clutching would accompany her fifteen years later to her college dorm room, in a future I could not even imagine on that snowy night. It was a future in which she would leave me, join her new roommates—a future in which I would be careful not to let her see my tears but in which I would weep quietly by myself in the car on the trip back home.

But in that long-ago moment, I held her tiny hand while she held her bear. I, too, had only one thing in my other hand: a single bag that held keys, wallet, laptop, cell phone, and a few precious photos I always kept close. In that moment, we had so very little. But because we had each other, we had absolutely everything.

The transformer fire was quickly extinguished, and the evacuation order was ultimately canceled. Within a week, everything returned to normal, and I have great memories of the camaraderie I shared with my neighbors as we lived without power for a few days. I also have a deep gratitude for the chaos of a night that began with a phone call to 911 and ended with everyone safe and sound. Sometimes that is not the case.

I am still sorting through the paradox of faith revealed to me that night. The things I thought I truly valued and held precious, kept on high shelves and away from rambunctious children and guests, will all one day turn to dust and ash. A lifetime of treasures, objects lovingly purchased and displayed, will all one day turn to dust and ash. But love endures. Love feels like a hand clasping your hand; an arm around your shoulder; a well-worn teddy bear that has soothed childhood fears. Love is when your sleepy child asks you calmly, "Where are we going?" as you wrestle her into her snowsuit in the middle of the night. Love is when you answer, "I don't know," and she still trusts you to figure it out, to keep her safe and warm. Love is knowing you are not alone even when it is time to go.

My faith—any faith, really—is a paradox. We believe what we cannot see. We worship One who cannot be known. We trust in that which is intangible. Our faith requires us, each day, to face uncertainties with little more than a teddy bear or purse to accompany us. Our faith requires a nakedness, vulnerability, and a stripping away of everything until we acknowledge the essence of who we are: creatures who cannot see even two minutes into our own future and who desperately need to know we are loved.

Confronting an evacuation in two feet of snow, with little more than the clothes on your back, distills your faith down to the bare bones. We can have peace in an uncertain future because we trust in the One who calms the storms raging outside us and also from within us. And we can leave for destinations and situations unknown because our trust is not in our own ability to weather the storm.

Leaving home in the middle of the night during a snowstorm is much like leaving a religious community you once loved but have now outgrown. Both require courage and a leap of faith into an uncertain future. But I am convinced that there is a point at which leaving is a more faithful act than remaining. It is possible to stay in a place so long that your own integrity is compromised and you begin to accept the unacceptable.

One Sunday morning years ago, I listened to my pastor spend forty-five minutes of his sermon decrying the "broken families" responsible for the downfall of today's society. I sat and listened carefully to his words, initially willing to give him the benefit of the doubt. I have heard many sermons, and I know that truth can cut like a sword. I know the power of conviction. I had heard sermons that challenged me, made me angry, or gathered me like the refiner's fire. Yet it was the preacher's description of "brokenness" that propelled me toward the depths of disillusionment and sadness that many others have felt within churches.

That day I listened as a shepherd, entrusted with the care of this group of believers, defined brokenness in terms of hierarchy and structure: who was present in a family and who was absent, who was the head of a family and who lacked that authority. I listened as a shepherd failed to survey the congregation of people before him, so transfixed was he on changing demographics that he refused to speak to our actual brokenness, wounds, and scars. Because every type of family must deal with brokenness and must search for restoration. The brokenness of sexual or emotional abuse, or the brokenness of harsh criticism and even harsher punishment, or the brokenness of parental indifference or childhood defiance: brokenness comes to gay families and straight families, single parents and married couples, the poor and the rich, adoptive parents and biological parents alike. The devastation of a daughter's drug use, the financial crisis of a recession, or an unexpected death can break any family. All families are broken in some way because all families consist of flawed human beings in need of healing. And all families find restoration and healing when they receive support, encouragement, and assistance.

This sermon blamed absent fathers, divorced women, queer people, feminists, and non-Christians for how the world was changing. All I could hear was someone wanting to hold on to an American dream that had never existed and a family structure that was never normative. As I sat there, knowing I would leave and never return, I thought about all the happy and healthy families I knew, including my own small family of two. The one thing they had in common was they looked like love in action. That was the common trait present in the rich diversity of all different kinds of healthy families, of all shapes and sizes: love expressed through how each person treated others. When love is missing from a family, or when love is absent from a sermon, people will walk away.

This had been my church home for several years—my first attempt to be a part of a multiracial, multiethnic congregation. Despite my best efforts, however, I had known for a long time that this place could never be my spiritual home, and this particular sermon distilled that for me. I did not know the process for leaving a church. Previously, moves required by schooling and jobs had always precipitated any change I had made from one congregation to another. In each case, I had left a church home reluctantly, and in each case, I had already found a place of community and belonging to which I planned to go—from a storefront church in a large city to a tiny congregation in a rural college town, for instance. Each time I had left those spaces, the church had prayed and anointed my head with oil, rejoicing with me as I headed to my next assignment. In each church, African American elders had profoundly believed in God's calling on my life, and so they had sent me with their blessing to the next state, the next school, and the next mission.

So I had no script for leaving a place that has become toxic to my soul and spirit. After all, if I had an eschatological hope of a heaven in which people from every tribe and nation would gather, how could I not at least try to be a part of a multiracial and multiethnic community on earth? For months, as I worshipped in this space, I could not put my finger on what was missing. Why did this church, with a membership reflecting what heaven may be, never feel like home?

It was only during that final sermon before I left that the puzzle pieces clicked into place. In the eyes of this pastor and this church, my daughter and I were broken vessels—not because we were sinners saved by grace but because we represented a social and racial demographic this white male pastor had identified as somehow deficient, inferior to the hierarchical and patriarchal model he embraced.

On the Sunday that I left, it was because God had given me a new revelation about family. I sat there and reflected on one brief moment in John 19:26–27, when Jesus speaks these words: "Woman, behold thy son!" And to his disciple John: "Behold thy mother!" While suffering on the cross, in anticipation of his death, Jesus relinquishes his filial duty to his mother, Mary. As the eldest son, Jesus would have been responsible for her continued well-being. Into the hands of one of his disciples, John, Jesus commits the care of the one he loved so dearly. Not even the approach of death can diminish the love and respect he has for the woman who ushered him into the world and nursed him at her breast. But this brief exchange at the foot of the cross reveals something deeper. It establishes a kinship bond between Mary, mother of Jesus, and John, to whom Jesus entrusts her care. It is not, as patriarchal culture would have demanded, the transfer of a woman from one male authority to another male authority. Instead, this move is a radical alteration of familial relationships. No longer will ties of flesh and blood be the only factors for participation in a divine lineage. Mary has a new son, and John has a new mother.

Mother and brother, sister and father: these are no longer simply terms of biological destiny but of right relationship. Kinship is transformed; family becomes a beloved community in which we are called to care for one another without respect to blood ties. There are no broken families in the beautiful kin-dom of God, in which mutual love and compassion are the foundation. Mary and John are part of a new family being established by the work of Jesus on the cross. The first act of this new family is to comfort each other as they grieve the Crucified One.

I had to leave that particular church because my life as a Black woman—one who had seen various permutations of family life—had given me a new Christology, a new understanding of how the work of the cross is a radical reordering and disruption of hierarchical models. The mismatched, ragtag family I had put together during my years of schooling and my years of academic life, and this beautiful daughter who was growing up beloved and affirmed, were all a reflection of God's divine love. The people willing to grieve with you at the foot of the cross are members of your family.

I discovered as I walked out of the doors of the church that morning that sometimes God's grace and our own growth are in leaving things behind.

※ ※ ※

My grandmother was among the generations of African Americans who left the rural South during the waves of the Great Migration. She would eventually end up in New York, while her family scattered to many of the receiving cities of these domestic refugees: Chicago, Philadelphia, and Los Angeles. I think about them, the millions of them, leaving behind beloved family members, leaving behind churches, leaving behind everything they had ever known, all for a promise—or even a mere hint of a possibility—of a better place ahead. Some left their Southern homes because they were forced to, because of the nightmare of American racism, including lynchings and threats of lynchings, cross burnings, and economic disenfranchisement. Some left willingly, because they had dreams of a better life somewhere else. Sometimes I sit with the collective weight of millions of people who had to ask themselves whether leaving was a better option than staying, or whether leaving was perhaps the only option on the table.

In his collection *Montage of a Dream Deferred*, Langston Hughes begins his poem "Harlem" with the famous question, "What happens to a dream deferred?" Hughes was a part of that great early twentieth-century renaissance of Black intellectual, cultural, and artistic expression that owed its existence to the waves of migrants from Southern cities. There is a mournfulness in Hughes's question, especially considering the unrealized potential of the millions who left the South but never found the American dream. They went to locations north and west, seeking the promised land of big cities and employment. These urban centers were supposed to be the escape from the Southern trees that bore such "strange fruit," as that haunting song first recorded by Billie Holiday goes—strange fruit with "blood on the leaves and blood at the root." To the North these massive waves of migrants went, looking for work outside of the system of sharecropping, slavery by a different name. And to the West they also went, seeking wide-open spaces and greener pastures and a chance to own their own land. They migrated hoping for jobs in factories and relief from the backbreaking toil of farming. They left the only homes they had known for generations, seeking not merely economic opportunities but an escape from the domestic terrorism of white supremacy.

But what happens when you travel for generations through the wilderness only to reach the promised land and find it is not the place you thought it would be? This is the question Hughes ponders in his poem: How does an entire group of people collectively experience a dream deferred? This dream of freedom, peace, and prosperity met the nightmare of continued Jim and Jane Crow, racial segregation, high rents, overcrowding, ghetto tenements, racial violence, and lynchings. My grandmother left the toil of the cotton fields of Georgia only to spend the vast majority of her adult life working in white women's kitchens. Did leaving Georgia mean simply trading one nightmare for another? What dreams were abandoned on those sharecropping fields she left behind? What nightmares did she encounter while scrubbing someone else's floors? What dreams were deferred in that Manhattan highrise, where her meager earnings were reduced each time she was sent home with a bag of hand-me-down clothing—as if somehow old clothes could pay her bills?

In her second definition of womanism, Alice Walker describes a womanist as a person who is "traditionally capable, as in: 'Mama, I'm walking to Canada and I'm taking you and a bunch of other slaves with me.' Reply: 'It wouldn't be the first time.'"

As a womanist theologian, I have to acknowledge that the act of leaving is a contradiction. In Walker's definition, it is a capable Black woman—that "strong Black woman" of both myth and reality—who is able to leave slavery and take other enslaved persons with her. This definition is meant to evoke the spirit of Harriet Tubman: her courageous escape from enslavement and her even more courageous decision to return to bondage on at least thirteen separate occasions to free others. Yet as capable and strong as Walker's definition suggests Black women are, leaving means walking away from people and places you love. Where is the space for strong Black women to acknowledge their weakness and their pain? Who is ready to actually listen to rather than minimize the hurt of strong Black women as they leave?

Enslaved women were forced to leave behind children who were torn from their breasts at the slave auction block. Some eventually had additional children and built new families, but when were they ever allowed to grieve for those taken from them? Some Black women bravely escaped enslavement, leaving behind parents and siblings—families who understood why their loved ones had to escape. But what about the pain of those who had to live with the consequences of these hard choices? Some Black women chose death over enslavement, leaving this mortal realm by jumping off the death slave ship or walking into the muddy waters of the Ibo Landing. Can we grieve at the horrific choice they had to make even as we celebrate their courage?

The experiences of Black women force us to ask, How do you live in the space of contradiction? What do you do when there is no reassurance that leaving is a better choice than remaining where you are?

When Alice Walker suggests in her definition of womanism that it "wouldn't be the first time," she is sensitive to the ways Black women today are still navigating the pain and the possibilities of leaving. Some Black women, after earning the highest degrees offered by the academy, leave spaces of power and privilege, choosing not to work in the toxic soup of higher education . . . and discover that the nonprofit and social justice agency worlds they have chosen come along with all the same hierarchies and racism. Some Black women leave the church, after finding little sanctuary but plenty of misogyny and patriarchy . . . only to find that their self-help books and yoga classes and meditation techniques fail to fill a deep spiritual void. Some Black women leave unhealthy relationships, breaking away from those who try to diminish them, those who try to dim their shine . . . only to find a life of loneliness, all the challenges of Black marriage demographics, and the possibility they may never meet a life partner.

Leaving is trusting in God. Leaving is a leap of faith with no guarantee that the situation you encounter once you have left will be any more life-giving. Leaving is walking out of Egypt without the certainty that you will ever arrive in Canaan. Leaving is accepting that you may be capable and strong but that your hurts as you walk out of the door are still very real. The lesson of leaving is not in the destination, which you may never reach, but in the journey itself.

On a snowy night, I was willing to leave my house knowing that as long as my child and I were safe, I had everything I needed; I believed that God would provide. But I also felt the weight of responsibility for keeping my child safe and warm, along with the profound loneliness of not knowing exactly where we would go. In leaving a church, I gained a more powerful understanding of the kin-dom of God—an understanding of the cross as a vehicle for forging relationships and ties with all who are members of the body of Christ. Yet I still fear that the multiracial church movement simply replicates racist hierarchies, patterning itself after the white supremacist society in which it is lodged.

Leaving comes at a cost. The best we can do, perhaps, is leave with dignity. We can strive to leave faithfully. For Black women who have left homes, relationships, churches, and burning houses with nothing but the clothes on their backs, there is honor in knowing they are part of a long legacy of women—women who walked to freedom and brought others along with them.

5　Holy Ghost(ly) Silences

*While we wait in silence for that final luxury of fearlessness,
the weight of that silence will choke us.*

—AUDRE LORDE

I made the mistake of speaking up in the faculty meeting. Passionate that new students should be exposed to some of the best minds in the discipline, I argued that seasoned and tenured faculty members should teach some of the first-year survey courses.

Which is how I found myself with a team of four teaching assistants, a Monday-Wednesday-Friday-morning teaching schedule, and a classroom filled with 150 first-year students. Almost all were between eighteen and twenty years of age, and for most of them, this was their first humanities course at the college level. I wanted to give them an introduction to the material they would never forget, so that semester I probably spent more time working on that class than the students did. And I learned never to suggest new ideas at faculty meetings.

A classroom can quickly become a community. You learn people's habits: where they sit and whether they arrive early or barely on time. You watch friendships form through group activities. In classes of first-year students, you literally watch some of the boys grow right before your eyes. While I understood that most students were taking the class to fulfill a general education requirement, there were a few I was certain would become majors in the discipline. The evidence was not just their written work but the way they engaged me during my lectures and in the discussion sections with the teaching assistants. Their bright and eager faces—and even the sleepy and hungover ones—served as a touchstone to remind me why I felt called to the teaching profession. Despite the workload and the logistical nightmare of it all, I was loving every minute.

On a Friday morning during the spring semester, one of my teaching assistants entered the classroom just as I was offering some preliminary remarks at the beginning of my lecture. He emphatically gestured to get my attention, and since students were still arriving and settling into their seats, I hurried to oversee the latest crisis. Was the overhead projector not working? An impending fire drill? The copy machine malfunctioning again?

A class this size had a lot of moving parts, and my teaching team and I had become a well-oiled machine, handling student conflicts, grade disputes, and the general minutiae of a large survey course. There was rarely a class period where some crisis failed to rise and meet us.

This particular teaching assistant was special. I was chair of his dissertation committee, and he was my only African American doctoral student. Despite having been given the options of an easier teaching assignment or even teaching his own class, he decided to help with this class instead. He was dedicated to walking with me throughout his educational journey, and I was honored to serve as his mentor. Because I knew him well and knew that student concerns did not scare him easily, the look on his face as I approached him gave me pause. Very quickly, before I could even ask what was wrong, he told me that four police officers were waiting outside the classroom. They said they needed to speak with me.

The physical configuration of that moment is forever burned in my memory. The only door to the classroom closed behind me, and my teaching assistant stood in front of it. I stood in the hallway directly between him and the four law enforcement officers. These were not the campus police who rode bikes and Segways around campus. These were armed municipal law enforcement officers from the small Southern city in which the university was located. I introduced myself and then asked them what they needed. They spoke quickly and quietly. They had a warrant for the arrest of one of my students. The registrar had given them the time and location of his class this morning. They needed me to either ask the student to step outside or allow them to enter the class and take him into custody.

The only way I can describe this moment was that I was outside of myself, as I spoke without a moment of hesitation or consideration. I told the officers that they could not enter my classroom. I informed them that the class would last fifty minutes. And I apprised them that only after I dismissed the rest of the students would I allow them to take the student into custody and that they could not set foot in my class. Without waiting for a response, I walked back into classroom, followed by my TA.

I walked to the podium and began my lecture. For fifty minutes, my teaching assistant stood silently in front of the door. The TAs usually sat together in the front row, but for the entirety of this class, he stood as silent witness and line of defense. He stood like any good church usher does, guarding the doors to the sanctuary so no one can enter or exit while the preacher is speaking.

I do not know whether my voice trembled as I lectured, but the classroom felt particularly quiet. I do not know whether any of the students overheard or saw the encounter outside of the classroom, but the usual noises of books being shuffled, snacks being unwrapped, conversations being whispered all seemed to be muted. I felt every movement and heard every noise during those fifty minutes, which seemed interminable and yet were all too quickly over. Near the end of the period, I moved to dismiss the students with various reminders for upcoming exams, readings, and instructions for discussion sections. And at the very end, I asked a young man to come and see me while the rest of the class filed out into the hallway.

He was a young Black man, a first-year student. His attendance had been sporadic, but when he did attend, he sat in the front of the classroom. In a sea of mostly white faces at a mostly white school with mostly white faculty, I knew his name, and I knew he was a smart kid. He approached my desk with a ready smile. I'm sure he was prepared to offer an excuse as to why he had missed a quiz or a discussion section. I quietly told him that four police officers were waiting outside to take him into custody. I explained that they had been waiting since the beginning of the class period and that I had not allowed them to come in and arrest him in front of the other students. I told him that I was waiting for everyone to leave and that now we would walk out together and face the situation.

I wanted to say more—words I didn't even have at the time. Words about dignity. Words that would comfort. But I had none. I just know that the Black professor, and the Black teaching assistant, and the Black student walked out of the door and faced four white police officers.

We were joined by my department chair, who must have been alerted to the situation and arrived while I was lecturing. I looked directly in the eyes of the police officer who had initially explained the situation to me. I thanked him for his patience, even as a different officer was placing handcuffs on my student. Then they escorted him out the door. Despite the fact that I followed up with the university registrar, at the police station, and at the local jail, I never heard from or saw that student again.

My all-too-brief encounter with this young man haunts me like a ghost. It haunts me like the son my womb longs for but has never conceived. I am haunted by the idea that I could have done more, or said more, or somehow magically conjured a better outcome.

My former teaching assistant, my silent witness and sentry, is now a tenured professor. Not long ago, when I was serving as a guest lecturer at his current institution, he reminded me about this story. He remembers the fear he felt as we dared to keep the officers out of our classroom community, not even knowing whether we had the legal right to do so. I actually cannot recall the fear, though I must have been afraid. I am, however, acutely pained by the lack of surprise in my student's eyes: his immediate resignation, his acquiescence to the news that he was going to be detained.

Above all, I remember the ghostly silence of the few seconds it took the three of us to walk into the future waiting outside my classroom door. Maybe he had already known they were coming to arrest him; maybe I was the only one out of the loop. Or maybe the silence housed inevitability: the inescapable fact of living in Black bodies in America. The haunting feeling that somewhere, someday, someone is coming for you.

Speaking into the silence is fraught with risk. We risk being misunderstood or misinterpreted. We risk ridicule and derision. It is scary to speak and to make our voices heard, and our fear often keeps us silent. I wanted to offer words of dignity and comfort to my student facing arrest, but I found myself strangely quiet. I wanted to rebuke and reprimand the law enforcement officers detaining him, but I feared repercussions for doing so.

Black feminist writer Audre Lorde reminds us most poignantly that our silence will not protect us. "I was going to die, sooner or later, whether or not I had even spoken myself," she writes. "My silences had not protected me. Your silences will not protect you . . . what are the words you do not yet have? What are the tyrannies you swallow day by day and attempt to make your own, until you will sicken and die of them, still in silence? We have been socialized to respect fear more than our own need for language."

What I most wanted to tell my student was that he was bigger and better than his worst mistake and that this particular setback did not have to define his life. But I failed to say it because, frankly, it rings hollow. Black children often are defined by their worst mistakes and are rarely given opportunities for redemption. Twelve-year-old Tamir Rice dared to play outside in a park with a toy gun in Cleveland, Ohio, and it cost him his life. Now, in hindsight, I wish I had told those police officers that coming to a young man's classroom to arrest him in front of his peers demonstrated they valued humiliation over justice. But I failed to say it because the hot sting of shame closed my throat. The weight of Blackness being seen as pathological silenced my words. When a whole race is under scrutiny, silence seems to make sense. Yet I failed to speak truth to power or offer comfort when it was most needed.

When to speak and when to be silent was a topic of much discussion in my grandmother's house. Children were expected to be silent unless an adult was talking to them. They were expected to be silent for hours and hours of church services, even as some services tarried overnight. And they were certainly expected to be silent at school, where model behavior was expected in front of mainly white teachers. The routine notation on my elementary school report cards—"talks too much in class"—led to many tears and punishments, along with the stern rebuke that the Holy Ghost needed to teach me when to speak and when to be silent.

Invoking the Holy Ghost was a serious matter in my childhood home, where, by tradition of the King James Version of the Bible, we used "Holy Ghost" rather than the "Holy Spirit" to refer to the third member of the Trinity.

The church women of my childhood taught me that the Holy Ghost was both Comforter and Disrupter. I witnessed, Sunday after Sunday, as the power of the Holy Ghost was called upon to soothe, heal, and comfort the afflicted and the broken. The Holy Ghost as Comforter was a gentleman, a sweet and gentle spirit. And yet the church mothers reminded me that the Holy Ghost was a Disrupter, too—a being who, through signs and wonders, unknown tongues and bodily praise, could disrupt a worship service or stop a sermon or bring forth an unsolicited testimony. These Black church mothers had a highly developed pneumatology—although that fancy academic term for the theology of the Holy Spirit would never have crossed their lips. They were true trinitarians. That is, the Holy Ghost was not the neglected stepchild of the Trinity, as it is throughout many ecclesial spaces; it was an active and engaged power. The gifts of the Spirit—including healing, miracles, prophecy, tongues, and the interpretation of tongues—were spiritual works that I regularly witnessed in my childhood. For those living on the underside of history, for the disenfranchised and dispossessed, for the "least of these," the Holy Ghost can supernaturally disrupt time and space and miraculously make a way out of no way.

As my grandmother prayed—loudly and in my presence—over each "talks too much in class" report card, she petitioned that I would receive discernment regarding when to speak and when to be silent, when to comfort and when to disrupt. While she never said as much, I have no trouble believing that she prophetically saw the woman I would become: someone who is compelled to speak truth even when her voice shakes. And because I am only now coming to terms with my grandmother's spiritual gifts, perhaps she could even foresee the future me that would be called to preach, teach, and lead institutions.

I regret not speaking the truth when my student was arrested. No consequence I may have faced equaled the gravity of a life interrupted at eighteen years old. I regret not challenging the forces, powers, and principalities that called for his arrest in front of a classroom filled with his peers. I regret my silence as I accompanied this young man outside the door into his radically transformed future.

Learning the difference between the ghostly silences into which we must speak truth to power and the holy silences from which we can draw strength and comfort may take a lifetime.

We sat by ourselves in a seminary classroom, a place set aside to train people for Christian ministry, where the faithful come to learn how to be effective leaders for the church. We sat side by side in the back, not in our usual professor and student places. I listened as you described how organized religion had failed you. I listened when you told me about the abuse you had experienced at the hands of those who were supposed to shepherd you. I shed tears as I listened to how you left the church, outraged over the politics that obscured the true teaching of the gospel.

I listened as you detailed the many ways that places of worship have truly failed to reach the lost, feed the hungry, and care for the least of these. I could only nod my head in agreement as you listed the ways that theology, religious doctrine, and human-made dogma have served to oppress, silence, and marginalize those already at the very fringes of society. I could not disagree with you, as you echoed the sentiments of Frederick Douglass and James Baldwin: if American Christianity, as it is typically practiced, was true religion, then you wanted nothing to do with it.

What could I say to combat the evidence you cited? False prosperity gospel doctrine does line the pockets of the preachers and empty the accounts of those least able to afford it. Protesters from various churches do carry signs declaring God's hatred of different groups. Pulpits and pews are full of those who are interested in personal piety to the exclusion of communal edification. I could not refute your facts. I kept silent and listened.

But in my heart, I wanted to shout that I was not that kind of Christian. There are millions of us who are not that kind of Christian. I wanted to tell you about the powerful saving grace I have experienced, which equips me to serve others with my whole being. I wanted you to know that so many Christians do not stop at the message of personal salvation but insist on an engaged, socially conscious, and vibrant faith. I wanted to tell you about all the people of integrity who would never abuse those in their flock—people who would lay down their very lives for those they serve. I wanted to tell you about the power of an institution that built the civil rights movement, feeds the hungry, clothes the naked, and cares for the widowed and the orphaned. I wanted to counter each of your examples with one of my own. I wanted to articulate a different theology and doctrine, detailing creeds that are liberating and affirming for the believer.

But I remained silent. In that moment, I needed to listen, not to speak. I needed to hear and understand your anger. I needed to accept my own complicity, both as a minister of the gospel and as a member of the Christian body. I remained silent so that I could attend to the full weight of your words. I resisted the urge to quickly refute your points without sitting with the impact of the truths you revealed, knowing that if I rushed to assure you I was not that kind of Christian, I would be minimizing the pain and anger you felt. I remained silent so that I could hear you, realizing that part of your anger was directed at the church's constant attempts to keep the discontented quiet.

I held your hand and we both cried tears, even as you accepted my embrace. My heart was full, and I almost—almost—uttered a clichéd but heartfelt phrase: "I'll pray for you." I stopped myself right before the words fell from my mouth because I knew that you had had enough of Christians praying for you. And so we sat in silence, holding hands and letting the tension and the anger exist—both for you and for me.

I am thinking of you today, hoping that in daring to speak these words, you experienced some healing. I was challenged by the truth of your words. I am thinking of you today, not from a zeal to change you but out of a godly love to hear you. I absolutely long for you to know God as I know God: to experience the love and grace of God's unconditional love. I long for you to separate a witness of genuine faith from those all-too-common examples of hypocrisy. If none of these are possible, I long for you to at least know that some of us care and that we listen.

There is a silence that is holy. There is a silence that is saving. There is a silence that is healing. There is a silence that allows others to be heard. There is a silence that is the presence of the precious Holy Ghost.

6 Being Present

Split a piece of wood; I am there. Lift up the stone, and you will find me there.

—GOSPEL OF THOMAS

As a new school board member tasked with spending time in various schools across our district, I was assigned to spend the day with Mrs. B. and her kindergarten class. She was a highly experienced teacher, having taught several different grades over twenty years, but she always chose to return to the youngest of students, her special calling. She welcomed me warmly when I entered, and I took a much-too-small seat at the back of her classroom to observe her class's routine. As each child arrived, Mrs. B. quietly marked their attendance on the daily sheet, which I dutifully delivered to the principal's office at her request. So I was surprised when later, after everyone had entered and put away their belongings in individually labeled cubbies, Mrs. B. took a formal roll call of her classroom. She called each child by their full name—first name, middle name, last name—their serious, grown-up government names, into which their little five-year-old bodies had yet to grow. Each student, clearly accustomed to this routine, answered her with a firm "Present!"

During our debriefing later that afternoon, I asked Mrs. B. why she took a verbal roll call, having already sent the official record of attendance to the principal. She shared her wisdom about this practice with me. When the children enter, they are still caught up in the moment of greeting their friends or leaving their parents. They are worried about their lunch or checking to see whether their favorite friends are at school. They are loud and distracted and unfocused on the task at hand. Mrs. B. related that she took a verbal roll call each and every day in order to focus their attention on her, their teacher and guide, and on the work they needed to do when they entered her classroom. When they settled down and answered "Present" to the calling of their names, Mrs. B. shared, she knew that they were ready, focused, and mentally available to begin a new day.

Thinking about her words as I drove home, I considered the many occasions when my body has shown up but I failed to be fully present. The modern condition is equal parts distraction and multitasking: We talk on the phone with our loved ones while we return emails. We text and check social media while we eat lunch. We drive distracted, with electronic and cellular devices and fifty-foot billboards grabbing our attention. Our attention is so divided at both work and home that we find it difficult to be fully present for one task at a time. We do multiple things at once but rarely any single thing well.

For just a few fleeting moments in Mrs. B.'s classroom, I watched five-year-olds respond with attention, respect, and awe as their teacher called their names. They knew their names were going to be called, and they knew a response was expected. This simple routine echoes the call-and-response tradition of the Black church context in which I was raised. The pastor or the worship leader or the speaker expects a response: an "Amen" or a "Preach!" or a "Yes, God." The response encourages the speaker; it affirms that those gathered are listening and that they are being uplifted by the words they hear. And those gathered in the pews need to know that they are seen—that the speaker knows how to move, shift, and change in response to their listeners. Speaker and listener both need each other during this dance of worship.

Mrs. B. confided in me that by the middle of the school year, the way in which a student answers "Present!" tells her everything she needs to know: whether this girl is sad or happy, whether that boy is excited about the day or longing for his mom or dad. She had learned to read the slightest intonations in the voices of her beloved students. And they had learned to trust her with their vulnerabilities. Her technique was old-school, but I understood its value. Everyone, no matter how fleeting the occasion, wants to feel seen and affirmed. Everyone wants to know that their presence matters: that someone knows their name, hears the tremble in their voice, and cares for them unconditionally.

I was sitting in the pulpit on Palm Sunday, and from that vantage point, I had a clear view of this particular African American congregation. I saw what I expected to see—what I knew I would see when I accepted the invitation to preach at this aging church in a troubled urban center. The congregation that gathered was around one hundred people, despite a facility large enough to accommodate five times that number and despite the hundreds of names on the official church roll. While there were a few young people under eighteen, the congregation was mostly over sixty-five. Only a handful of men, including the two ministers who sat in the pulpit with me, were present. The facility was well cared for and scrubbed clean, but it was showing its age. The words appearing on plaques below the stained-glass windows and on the sides of the pews reflected the names of church members and families who had passed away long ago. I was in a historically Black city, an urban church, and a neighborhood ravaged by the twin beasts of gentrification and displacement.

I have been in the pulpits of small Black Baptist churches across the country, so everything in this particular sanctuary was a familiar sight: a decline in membership; an aging church population unable to attract young families; a desire to fight the hostile developers vying for church property but a lack of resources to do so; and a congregation of people who could barely afford to live in the neighborhoods in which their families had lived for generations. Some would argue that these aging churches are places of death, connected to the overall decline of Christianity in America. The statistics tell the story—even within the deeply religious African American context, participation and membership in traditional church bodies are in decline.

Yet somehow, in the midst of these realities, the preacher of the hour is called upon to offer a few words of life and hope, of resuscitation and resurrection. In that very moment, in that particular pulpit, I felt overwhelmed by the task before me: bringing a word from God to the people of God. I had recently moved to Washington, DC, where the disappearance of Black churches in a formerly majority African American city was apparent even during the short time I had lived there. I feared for the fate of this small church in whose pulpit I was now sitting.

But then.

A deacon—his face carved with lines and memories of things he could not forget—approached the altar and began a prayer of intercession. His firm voice called on the God of Abraham, Isaac, and Jacob. He petitioned the Rock, the cornerstone that the builders rejected. His prayers anointed that small sanctuary, and the presence of God filled the place.

I watched as a pair of frail hands lifted themselves up high in worship. Dressed in her Sunday best with a wide-brimmed hat, this older woman stood with hands uplifted even as tears streamed down her face. She, too, was at the throne of grace. Prayers both private and corporate joined together. The words were indistinguishable, but all our hearts gathered together for this moment of congregational prayer.

On that Sunday morning there was music and dance, and there was laughter and sorrow. Announcements were read and scripture was proclaimed. The choir sang, and grandbabies cried. The service may have looked like chaos to the outsider, but it was a carefully orchestrated symphony to the initiated. As I brought forth the Word, my message seemed insufficient, my ideas too simplistic. I only had a few feeble words about a God who sees us, a God who knows us by name, who calls us into ourselves, like a beloved kindergarten teacher calling her students to order. Those same frail hands and lined faces responded to my words and lifted me higher. They encouraged and pushed; they called and responded. As I spoke, one elder simply stood silently with his arms folded. He did not contribute to the shouts of "Amen!" or "Yes, daughter." He simply stood in affirmation, a silent and seemingly unmovable witness. His praise language was not a shout or a dance; he was not a musician or a singer. He just stood perfectly still, a serious expression on his face. Somehow, seeing him, I felt stronger and bolder.

In that small church, in a neighborhood that stimulus funds neglected, a great cloud of witnesses in this realm and beyond worshipped with a truth and intensity that moved my soul. This church was a place of life, not death. It may have been aging, but it was not yet dead. It was a stark reminder that small things, seemingly insignificant places, can be alive and well despite pronouncements of decline. Members of the church were raising grandchildren whose parents had been lost to the prison industrial complex. The congregation awarded small scholarships to graduating seniors, even as few of the elders had ever attended college themselves. They took time to pray for the sick and to visit the shut-ins, thus filling in the gaps of a racially biased health-care system. As a church body, they were a balm for the lonely and the unloved, a respite for the aging and the forgotten. In these small churches, never destined to grow into massive sanctuaries with professionally produced cable programs and revenue-generating online broadcasts, God was still moving.

What I have witnessed in small, aging, and even declining churches across the nation is that true worship distills the power of death and restores life. Healing and joy and catharsis and fellowship and music and laughter and singing are all life-giving. On Sunday mornings, in thousands of unassuming places across this country, there are moments of true worship in which spirit and truth restore the breath of life to those who far too often live on the edges of death. True worship begins first with us showing up and being fully present in the moment. As noisy and chaotic as that small church may have seemed, sitting there in worship with them was the first time that week I had felt connected and seen—not just in my role as the preacher for the morning but as a beloved daughter of God.

❧ ❧ ❧

To be present in worship is to bring our full selves into the process. Worship involves our minds being open and receptive to the wisdom of the Word. Yes, worship means being open to the explication and theology of the scholar, but also being open to the common sense of the great cloud of witnesses who have walked before us. Yes, it means our minds being open to the theological nuances of our faith, but also ever leaning on the Everlasting Arms.

As a womanist theologian, I affirm that worship involves our physical bodies being fully present: the lifting of the hands, the tapping of the feet, the standing in affirmation, the shaking of the head, and even the running around the sanctuary. Worship is the joyful acknowledgment that this broken vessel of a body is yet wonderfully and fearfully made in the image of God. When we are fully present in worship, we focus our attention on the One who has made us, the One who sustains us.

When we are fully present in mind and soul and body, we embrace worship as a time of praise and thanksgiving as well as a time of lament and mourning. When we are fully present in worship, we participate in a creative theological process, daring to both raise and answer questions about the nature and reality of God. Theological work cannot simply take place in academic spaces; it is not a dry set of questions to be posed by those who are "qualified," those who have a set of particular educational credentials. You do theology in community, and the best the-ology reflects the cares and concerns of that community. This theology often shows up in sermons, songs, and praises.

In that small Baptist church where I was the invited preacher for Palm Sunday, the choir sang "Were You There (When They Crucified My Lord)?" That beloved spiritual caused me to reflect theologically on the power of showing up and on the experience of the radical presence of God the song embodies. We hear both grief and praise in the plaintive question of this spiritual, coined by some unknown enslaved person who dared to transcend their suffering and to enter, fully present, into this ultimate experience of worship.

For the question "Were you there when they crucified my Lord?" is not a historical one but a theological one. More than two thousand years removed from the reality of Jesus's crucifixion, this spiritual does not look backward to the eyewitnesses of the cross. Instead, it stresses the reality of the current moment by daring to ask the listener, "Were you there?" With this emphasis on "you"—on those of us who could not have been physically present—it reminds us that the believer still needs to show up at the foot of the cross and to identify with the radical act of Jesus's death and resurrection. The song does not ask whether your father or your brother or your sister or your mother was there but whether you were there—whether you have indeed reflected on the sacrifice embodied by the cross.

This anonymous songwriter—this enslaved person whose legal and material status was less than human—penned this spiritual about a space of suffering and anguish, a space of questioning and despair, a space of "Why, oh God, have you forsaken me?" Yet this spiritual also affirms that there is victory over the grave; there is the possibility of resurrection in death-defying places. People of African descent could never have survived four hundred years of chattel bondage without believing in the possibility of life even in spaces of death. There is fullness of life when you show up, fully present, when people are suffering and where people are bearing the burdens of their own crosses. "Were You There" is a reminder that to be fully present with the whole of humanity does not require us to enter the sanctuary or walk across the threshold of a church. The cross, Calvary, is a site of public spectacle. The rhetorical question "Were you there?" signifies the real, pressing question about whether you will be present for lost and hurting generations.

To be present is to be wherever there is need. Were you there when the levees broke during Hurricane Katrina or when the earthquake shook Haiti? Will you be there when the next natural disaster strikes and the most vulnerable cannot find shelter?

To be present is to sit with those who grieve; it is to offer no clichés of comfort but simply the presence of your love. Were you there when Trayvon Martin was murdered and Black mothers throughout the country were grieving? And will you be there when the next unarmed child is killed by those sworn to protect and serve?

To be present is to be where people are suffering. Were you there among the hungry and the homeless, those in search of both their spiritual and physical daily bread? Will you be there on those street corners and back alleys, where the walking dead are in need of a healing touch? Or will you cross to the other side of the street?

To be present is to be at the front lines of the fight for justice. Were you there in Selma and Birmingham, risking the dogs and the water hoses? Will you be there on Capitol Hill to fight for health care for the uninsured? Will you be there at your senator's office to protest the cuts to educational funding even as another several billion dollars are appropriated to fight unjust wars?

The lyrics of "Were You There" continue with the words "Oh, sometimes it causes me to tremble! Tremble! Tremble!" I wonder whether we have lost our ability to tremble—to be deeply affected—in the face of injustice. I wonder whether we no longer tremble in the presence of a holy God who requires us to do the work of justice. In our comfort and ease, we no longer tremble at the pain, passion, and sacrifice of Calvary.

Another one of my enslaved forbearers penned some poetic words in a different spiritual about a "great gettin' up morning": that day in which a final roll will be taken, when all will have to give an account of their lives. On that day, we all will have to firmly answer "Present!" when the divine calls our names. How will our presence, or our absence, at all the public spectacles of suffering and injustice be judged by a God who stands firmly on the side of the oppressed?

7 Tender Love

Oh Mary, don't you weep / Tell Martha not to moan / Pharaoh's army drowned in the Red Sea / Oh, Mary don't you weep / Tell Martha not to moan.

—African American spiritual

Having an office you do not have to share is a blessing. An office with a door that closes and locks—a door on which you can hang a sign that says "grading" or "on a conference call"—gives assurance that people will not disturb you. I acknowledge the blessing of that private room with a locking door, the blessing of being able to cry in private.

This time I did not have to cry in the bathroom like I did last time, hiding my heaving sobs by flushing the toilet so that

I did not make the woman in the stall next to mine uncomfort-able. (She heard me anyway.) This time I did not have to run to my car, hoping that the tears would wait to fall until I could shut and lock the door of my vehicle, until I could park under a tree away from the doors of the stores. (The floodgates started before I even put the key in the ignition.) This time I did not have to bite my lip to keep from crying in public, or snap the hairband on my wrist to keep me from forming those four-letter words that I have been trained not to utter.

No, this time I shut the door. Pressed the lock firmly. Sat down in my comfortable, ergonomically designed chair. And I cried. Overwhelmed and exhausted, I cried those so-very-tired kind of tears. These were the tears of someone with a nameplate outside her office and multiple letters behind her name. These were the tears of someone with a retirement plan and health insurance, the tears of the well dressed and well fed. These were the tears of someone who had done everything right and who everyone assumed had it all together. Yet the salty bitterness of tears tastes the same wherever you cry.

Because microaggressions sting like a thousand paper cuts. There are the small ways your work is dismissed and belittled, and all the tiny acts of disrespect and disregard. You are seen, but you are somehow still invisible. You are hypervisible and yet constantly silenced. These small cuts wound, and those wounds weep. And you realize, again and again, that your education or experience or expertise will not protect you from the racist and sexist jabs that undermine your confidence and authority.

So sometimes you cry. In your beautifully appointed office at an Ivy League institution—a place your enslaved ancestors built, brick by brick, but could not legally attend—you sit and you cry. Overwhelmed by the weight of four hundred years of white supremacist evil still active in the world, you cry.

"What are you crying about?" is a question from my childhood. Short of death or significant blood loss, crying was for the weak. You were not supposed to cry when spanked, or when death visited, or when injuries wounded. You could cry at church or in prayer, when presumably the power of the Holy Spirit overwhelmed you with its presence. But to cry at home, out of vulnerability or anger or the general unfairness of life, was unacceptable. It was reinforced to children, again and again. You have food, clothing, and shelter; why are you crying? Life is unfair; why are you crying? People are going to tease you and make fun of you; why are you crying?

I now understand my elders' attempt to impose a toughness on us, to prepare us for a life in which tears were seen as weakness. And I understand their desire to instill strength and grit into little Black children, to make us ready for the world outside our loving homes and churches. We were taught to be strong in the Lord and in the power of God's might. We were encouraged to be bold and brave in our faith, unashamed of the gospel. We were given warrior language and words such as *battle* to prepare for the upcoming fights against forces and principalities and powers. Those church mothers constantly drilled in us the importance of putting on the full armor of God, offensive and defensive weapons at the ready.

They were absolutely right. I still draw upon their lessons for the realities of living in this country, in this Black woman's body. I also understand my elders' toughness as a mechanism for dealing with poverty, and for living in a nation in which poverty is seen as a moral failure. The poor literally cannot afford to cry over the daily realities of life.

I have a very old scar on my finger, now folded into the wrinkles of my skin and almost invisible to everyone else, even though I can still trace its outline. It was the kind of injury that should have landed me in the emergency room for multiple stitches and antibiotics. But it is a wound of childhood poverty, in which everything short of death was handled in the family bathroom with Band-Aids, home remedies, prayer, and ointments. I remember choking back tears as my grandmother dressed this deep cut, prayed over it, and sent me back to whatever task was at hand.

But along the way—between putting on armor and getting ready to fight, amid choking back tears from real injuries and pain—no one managed to teach me that some situations call for gentleness and tenderness with yourself, since the world is never likely to be gentle and tender with you. I have been left wondering whether my own grandmother and the church women who raised me had the capacity to teach me about a tenderness that they themselves may never have experienced.

This raises for me a theological question I wrestle with to this day: Can Black women ever truly love God if we have never been taught to love ourselves? How do we love the One we cannot see if we are never taught to love ourselves and the very bodies we inhabit?

The first thing I noticed about the little girl on the bus was her hair. She had cornrows braided tightly on each side of her head so that they formed two pigtails on either side, with the requisite matching beads at the end. That is how my grandmother braided my hair for far too long, well beyond the age when I should have still been in ponytails and beads. My braids were my grandmother's signal to the outside world that I was still a vulnerable child despite my emerging woman's body.

I smiled and waved at the little girl and she smiled back, revealing missing top teeth. She was sitting patiently with her mother, dangling legs that did not reach the floor, wearing flip-flops with flowers on the top that matched her summer shorts set. I was sitting close enough to hear the noise made by her flip-flops, the up-and-down rhythm of her shoes hitting the back of her feet. And I was close enough to hear the warning from her mother to stop making all that noise.

On a city bus, ambulance sirens, car alarms, angry honking, loud conversation, and blaring music make the sound of tiny flip-flops completely inconsequential. Yet the young mother kept admonishing her child to be quiet. Stop making noise. Sit still. The girl stayed immobile for a few moments after the harsh reprimand, but then her five-year-old body went back to what a five-year-old body naturally does: move and make noise. Yes, I could hear exhaustion in this mother's voice, the grind that is parenting and public transportation and city life, the particular stress of parenting a young and active child. But I also watched this little girl shrink a little bit each time she heard the heat and the anger in her mother's voice. I heard the escalation of a mother's demands. Every word was a rebuke, a complaint, an admonishment, until finally came a hard pinch from the mother and a young daughter's tears, followed by "Stop with all that crying!"

She was a well-groomed, well-behaved, quiet child, who, I had no doubt, was also well loved by a mother who had the responsibility of teaching her some hard life lessons. But my heart longed for someone to speak to this baby girl softly and tenderly. Where will she, and so many others like her, learn that they deserve tender treatment and soft words? Where will she learn to love herself and to treat herself gently?

Will she grow up to be the woman who cries in her office at the news of the death of a loved one, wipes away the tears, and immediately goes back to work? Will she grow up to be the woman who faces surgery one day and insists the next day that she can drive herself home because she does not want to inconvenience anyone? Will she grow up to be the woman suffering from fibroids so painful that she can barely walk but still insisting on cooking Sunday dinner for her extended family?

Can Black women learn tenderness for the self when they need to provide so much care for others? Can Black women learn tenderness for the self within a faith that glorifies suffering?

Does God love Black women?

Statistics reveal the crushing inequality that marks Black women's lives in the United States. More than one-quarter live in poverty, a rate more than double that of their white counterparts. Black babies face double the risk of dying before their first birthdays as white babies do, and Black women are two to three times more likely to die from pregnancy-related causes than white women. Black women are significantly more likely to be the sole wage earner in their households; to never marry at all; to suffer divorce; or to be widowed young. Black women, even the most educated, struggle with housing insecurities at high rates and significant wage disparities. Black women are incarcerated at twice the rate of other women and face higher rates of death from treatable and preventable diseases. Despite pursuing post-secondary education at the highest rates in the nation, becoming entrepreneurs and business owners in unprecedented numbers and finally breaking through corporate, ecclesial, and academic glass ceilings, Black women still face underemployment, poverty, disease, and loneliness. Black women are still paid sixty-two cents for every dollar that a white man makes.

And yet Black women are among the most faithful and religious Americans by any measure. We attend church more frequently than people of any other race and more frequently than Black men. We pray more, give more, and serve more. We open the doors of the church, clean the bathrooms, and then close the doors of the church. With membership that is on average 85 percent female, Black churches across the nation rely on our tithes and our offerings to literally keep the lights on. We consistently indicate that faith is the most important aspect guiding decisions in our daily lives.

So how can we reconcile the stark contrast between Black women's material existence and our demonstrated love for God and faithfulness to God's people? I have never doubted, not even once, that the Black women in my life truly love God with all their might. I have sometimes doubted, however, whether God loves these faithful Black women in return. Even accepting the theological tenet that it rains on the just and unjust, that bad things happen to good people, I could not understand why such a disproportionate share of suffering seemed to be the lot of Black women. Why did it appear that the more faithful a Black woman was in her service to God, the more she suffered?

I was not allowed to voice such questions as a child. To question God's love and God's faithfulness was to be pointed to the sacrificial work on the cross. Of course, I was told, God loves us—just look at the sacrifice of God's only Son! I was reminded that no matter the material conditions of Black life, God's steadfast love can never be in doubt. Still, I had questions that I dared not speak: In the space of so much suffering, pain, and loss in Black women's lives, where was God? Where was God's love that was gentle, tender, and kind for those who have often only known harsh words? For those who have been told that they are ugly, inferior, undesirable, unmarriageable, angry, violent, promiscuous, and unwanted—the message that Black women receive from every media outlet and even from the pulpits of our own churches—I wondered where God's love appeared. I needed answers to my questions about God's love and tenderness in order to continue believing in God's faithfulness.

I found many of my answers not so much at the foot of the cross and the suffering found there as in the tenderness of a brown-skinned, scared, expectant young mother tending her baby.

✿ ✿ ✿

It is a curious thing to be a Protestant Pentecostal and yet somehow develop a high doctrine of Mary. Mariology, the theology surrounding the mother of Jesus, is generally a Catholic domain. Yet it is Mary, the mother of Jesus, who calls me to a new theological understanding of God loving the "least of these."

Mary's story was often an afterthought in the church of my childhood. She was seen as a minor actor, a bit player in the story of Jesus's life, death, and resurrection. We want to move so quickly to the outcome of her birth story—the arrival of God-with-Us—that we fail to spend sufficient time on the material, social, and spiritual condition of Mary herself. And while the patriarchal culture of her time records few details about her life, the biblical text gives us a few insights into the beauty and pain of Mary's story.

Theotókos. Mary is called in Greek: the "God-bearer." She is an unwed, pregnant teenager. Given those circumstances, there's a very real possibility that she would become a social outcast upon the news of her miraculous pregnancy—not simply that her fiancé would "put her away," but that the entire community in which she was raised would turn its back on her. How many of her relatives and friends fail to believe the extraordinary news concerning the conception of her child—not simply that Jesus is the promised Messiah but that she has conceived a child while still a virgin? In a culture in which a young woman belongs to either her father or her husband, God alters the course of Mary's life without notification or consultation with either.

And why do we fail to reverently pause in the story when the angel appears to Mary and attempts to reassure her with the words "Do not be afraid"—or, as some translations render it, "Fear not"? Why do we not take seriously the idea that Mary is terrified to find out she has been chosen for this momentous task, which she has neither sought nor requested? What if the angel's words are not mere reassurance but acknowledgment that anyone in this circumstance would tremble in fear?

We love to preach that Mary was blessed and highly favored to be chosen for this assignment, but we never preach on the fear, doubt, uncertainty, and confusion she must have surely felt even if she fully consented to this journey. When so many women during her time period failed to even survive childbirth, Mary was facing a season of both a new life growing inside of her and her possible death. We love to preach about the also-pregnant Elizabeth speaking life over Mary's womb in Luke 1:42: "Blessed is the child you will bear." But can we also imagine Elizabeth, with her own impending labor, blessing the child neither she nor Mary were guaranteed to live long enough to see?

When I take the story of Mary seriously, I find space for a Mariology that does not need to make an idol out of Mary nor to diminish the salvific work of Christ. Mary was fully human, and her cares and concerns echo those of women everywhere, particularly those of Black women. Black women, like Mary, have always faced ostracism and loneliness in our culture, whether it is our single-parent status, divorce rates, or never-married statistics. Black women have always had to live with the burden of fear, facing disproportionate rates of violence and homicidal deaths at the hands of those both within and outside our own communities. Black women have always dealt with the possibility of early death in terms of both maternal outcomes and infant mortality. Black women have always lived with untreated pain due to low rates of health insurance and racial bias in the health-care system. Black women have always known what it means to bring children into a nation in which you fear for your child's life. And like Mary, far too many Black women know the pain of an unjust and corrupt legal system and of state-sanctioned executions.

As I sit with Mary's story, I find the tenderness I was seeking as I tried to reconcile suffering and faithfulness. I find a woman who cradles her newborn son, feeds him from her own breast, and experiences the joy of his safe delivery even as she fears for his future. I find a woman whose cries and labor pains deliver the first news of the Word made flesh—the joyous news of the Savior of the world but also the painful anticipation of the sacrifice he will have to make. In Mary's story, I find a woman daring to believe in the impossible, even in the face of her own or others' doubts. Her fear does not keep her from magnifying the Lord.

And her fear helps to clarify for me how so many Black women, despite their material conditions and doubts and fears, continue to sing songs of thanks and praise. Black women hold on to the promise of Mary's song: that God will remove the mighty from their seat, exalt the humble and meek, fill the hungry with good things, and send the rich away empty.

A focus on Mary keeps me from immediately rushing to the passion of Christ, to the blood, the beatings, the nails, the excruciating death. As a Christian believer, I must go to the cross, for it is the heart of my faith. But in Christ's life for thirty-plus years, there was also a beloved mother who birthed and fed a child, cradled him in her arms, shared laughter, and sang her heart's song. There is a tenderness to Mary's story that gives me hope. Yes, Mary is present for Jesus's painful birth and his painful death. But there is also Mary, the mother who rocked her infant to sleep, watched her child take his first steps, and presented her son to the temple. She loved her child not because he suffered but despite all the suffering she knew he would endure.

My prayer is that Black women find a faith in a God whose love is not predicated upon superhuman endurance of systematic injustice. We are beloved daughters in need of a tender love and gentle mercy that is given as freely and abundantly as that of a mother.

8 A Question of Safety

*Are you sure, sweetheart, that you want to be well? . . . Just so's
you're sure, sweetheart, and ready to be healed, cause wholeness is no trifling matter. A lot of weight when you're well.*
—Toni Cade Bambara, *The Salt Eaters*

The wind, hail, and rain were so strong they shook the car. I
gripped the steering wheel and gave thanks that I was less than
five miles from my destination. Even in the safety of my vehicle,
I was stressed about the power of this storm and the possible danger I was in while driving through it. What had started off as a
sunny autumn morning in the South was now an early-afternoon
monsoon, and I was glad to be almost there. Almost there: the
point in your journey where you say to yourself, "If something

goes wrong and the car stops, I'm close enough to walk." My shoulders and arms ached from concentration, from the tension between wanting to drive faster to get there more quickly and needing to drive slowly to avoid the downed branches.

Suddenly, out of the corner of my eye, I saw movement on the shoulder of the road. Something deep within my spirit knew that it wasn't another branch or even a downed power line. I slowed my car even more and was surprised to see a woman pushing a stroller. In a few seconds, the brain can process so many disparate thoughts, trying to arrange what it sees into a narrative that makes sense. While she had an umbrella and the stroller had a plastic cover, there was no way she and her baby weren't completely drenched. Because of the fierceness of the wind, her umbrella was more hindrance than help, and the diaper bag hanging from the handles of the stroller was soaked.

This was a small Southern town, so I knew there was no public transportation for which to wait; you either walked or you drove. I had driven this stretch of road many, many times, and I knew there wasn't any shelter except for a gas station about two miles ahead. She was on the side of the road, and there was no safety ahead of her and no safety behind her. What I remember most were those tiny shoes peeking out from the stroller's ineffective plastic cover.

As I inched closer to the red light at an intersection, I had two sets of questions. The obvious questions revolved around what this woman was doing out in the storm. What dangers, seen and unseen, had sent such a vulnerable duo into the elements? Had the storm caught her off guard? No one willingly sets out on foot in the middle of a storm unless tempestuous weather is a better choice than staying.

My second set of questions should have been simpler, but they turned out to be the more complicated: Do I offer her a ride? I am a daughter of the church—a teacher, preacher, and follower of Christ. How could I see someone in need and not stop? About a month prior to this encounter, I had preached a sermon about the Good Samaritan, the parable whose simple lesson is that everyone we encounter is our neighbor, and we are commanded to love our neighbors.

But I am also a Black woman in America, whose life and experiences are a product of a complicated racial history. The woman on the side of the road, pushing her baby stroller in the torrential downpour, was white.

While waiting at the light, I thought a thousand different thoughts. None of them, in that moment, had anything to do with my own personal safety. I didn't wonder whether this woman was a murderer or a thief. I didn't speculate whether she had a bomb in her stroller instead of a baby. What I was most concerned about was whether *I* would be perceived as the threat—whether I would become the object of her fear. Would this woman, a stranger to me, be afraid of a Black woman pulling up beside her

and asking if she needed a ride? And what would she do out of
that fear? The pervasiveness of racism in this nation means that I
have been taught all my life to put white comfort ahead even of
my own safety. "Will she be afraid of me?" was my first thought—
long before I wondered whether I should be afraid of her.

It is a privilege not to have to factor race into the daily decisions you make, even your attempts to be a decent and moral
person. It is a privilege not to consider how race determines
whether you will be seen as the Good Samaritan or as the thief.
I think of the myriad ways I contort my body so that I am not
the object of white fear. When I go shopping, I try to shrink my
body; into stores I take nothing but my wallet, trying to silently
convey the message, "I'm not here to steal. I just need to shop."
In places where I am a stranger, I smile a bit more brightly and
give reassuring looks: "I was invited; no need to worry about
me." In the halls of power and privilege, where I am a regular
guest, my body sometimes wants to cry out, "Look at my hall
pass! I am here legitimately."

In so many spaces and in so many ways, I temper my voice
to speak more softly so I am not perceived as the angry Black
woman. I laugh and smile even when I don't want to so people
don't find me frightening or intimidating. I constantly think
about how to mitigate white fears of Black bodies because there
are dangerous repercussions for those who don't perform in the
ways that whiteness demands.

I fear that a wrong performance in front of a police officer will land me in jail or with a gun drawn and held to my head. I fear that a wrong performance in front of my white colleagues will result in a negative tenure review or the pulling of a book contract. I fear that failure to correctly perform Black womanhood in ways that whiteness deems acceptable will cancel the legitimacy of my work, my education, my credentials, and my humanity.

In his book *Whistling Vivaldi: How Stereotypes Affect Us and What We Can Do,* psychologist Claude Steele shares the story of *New York Times* columnist Brent Staples. As a young Black man, Staples learned to whistle Vivaldi concertos and other pieces of classical music to signify that he's not a threat as he walks the streets. He lives in a world in which white women clutch their purses and cross the street to avoid Black and brown bodies.

And so as I sat at the traffic light that afternoon, prepared to roll down my window and offer a white woman some respite from a storm, all I could think was, *What is the right song to whistle? What are the code words to demonstrate that I am not a threat?* Even at this critical juncture, I knew that my anxiety wasn't about this particular woman but about a lifetime of having to prove that, as a Black woman, I am also made in the image and likeness of God.

The traffic light turned green. Instead of going, I paused in indecision and then rolled down the front passenger-side window. Immediately, I was assailed by the wind blowing heavy rain over to the driver's seat. I leaned as far to the right side as I could and asked, "Are you okay? Do you need a ride?" She paused and our eyes connected. I could hear the baby's cries even over the noise of the downpour. After an eternal second, she silently shook her head no.

I tried to fill in the gap between us. I reassured her that there was a gas station a little over a mile up the road where I could drop her off. I asked her if there was anyone I could call to come and get her. I asked again if she was okay. She began to once again move forward with her rain-soaked stroller.

I played the only card I had left. "Please look," I said. "I have a car seat in the back. I'm also a mom. Please let me help you." In that moment, I poured out the oil in my alabaster jar, offering the thing that was most sacred to me. If she had been a murderer or a terrorist, I had just revealed the only weapon that could be used against me. Somewhere, out of the danger of this storm, I also had a beloved child.

I frantically pressed the button to open the backseat window so that she could see it was true, that there was a safe ride for her baby. And for a fraction of a second, I thought her eyes veered to the car seat, scanning this car empty of threats, before she met my eyes again. Then she spoke to me for the first time: "I'm fine."

While this entire encounter may have lasted only a minute, it felt like an eternity. I rolled up the windows and slowly drove away, continuing to note their progress in the rearview mirror.

I would like to offer a happier ending to this meeting at the side of the road. I wish I could conclude by saying that a grateful woman accepted my offer. I want to be able, when I share this story from pulpits and on pages, to say that she and I are still in touch. But that is not how the story ends. I cannot claim definitively that she rejected my offer because of my race, but this story is actually not about her refusal. This moment, this sharp pain I feel when I remember that long-ago afternoon, is about the mental and physical gymnastics that being Black in America has required of me. This story is about how exhausting it is to constantly convince others that you are not a threat, that the skin the Creator endowed you with is not a crime.

I often wonder how this woman remembers our shared story. I'm sharing my own memory: that of a woman trying to live out her ethical commitments despite the risks to her personal safety. Does the woman on the side of the road remember it differently? Did her friends hear a tale of a near kidnapping, a stranger's threat, a shadowy figure? Does her version of the story reinforce the idea of Blackness as a threat?

The lens of race shapes how we understand the murder of Eric Garner at the hands of a white police officer: as a reasonable punishment for selling untaxed cigarettes or as a lynching.

I know too much about American history to feel confident that one white woman and one Black woman viewed a shared encounter through the same lens. African American poet Lucille Clifton describes this complexity of racial history well in her short poem "Why Some People Be Mad at Me Sometimes" when she writes that people want her to remember their memories instead of her own—"and i keep on remembering / mine."

I keep on remembering the weariness I felt when I finally arrived home, still burdened with the image of baby shoes peeking out from a covered stroller. I keep on remembering my attempts to reassure, to shrink, to dispel fear. I keep on remembering that I cared more about this one stranger's child than this nation would ever care about the millions of Black and brown children whose safety, as they navigate a racist world, is always under threat. I embrace the womanist wisdom of Lucille Clifton's poem; I'll keep on remembering my memories, my stories, my pain, my discomfort . . . because no one else will.

Are you saved? That was the question my grandmother and the church mothers posed to strangers as they passed out religious tracts on the streets of Brooklyn. It was the question they asked church visitors whose salvation status was unknown. It was the question they posed to family members of the backslidden and the transgressors. "Are you saved?" By which they meant, "Do you know Jesus Christ as your personal Savior for the remission of your sins?"

Insiders to our Holiness-Pentecostal tradition know the correct answer to that question: "Yes, I'm saved, sanctified, Holy Ghost filled and fire baptized." To be saved by the blood of Jesus, to have a personal relationship with God, these were the limits of the soteriology—the doctrine of salvation—I encountered as a child. I was taught that if I could answer yes to the question of salvation, eternal life would be my reward. This limited understanding of salvation led me to believe that being saved is only about the individual: my relationship with God, my reward of heaven, my life being spared from the fiery pits of hell.

I had questions even then about this individualistic understanding of salvation. What good was it if I was saved but everyone else was lost? How did my salvation benefit those around me? And was the personal reward of eternal life sufficient when so many people I knew were already living in hell?

I needed a soteriology that had the entire community I loved, and not just the individual believer, at its core. Almost everyone I knew could answer affirmatively about their spiritual salvation, and yet almost everyone I knew struggled with the realities of Black poverty in the inner city. I needed to ask a different question than the one being posed by my church mothers.

After spending time with the Greek lexicon, I learned that the word *saved* can also be translated as "made whole," or "healed," or "preserved." I thus found the question I most needed to ask of both myself and others was, What must I do to be safe? This question transformed my soteriology by wedding together Jesus's concern for both our spiritual and material conditions.

How can fractured communities and broken people be made whole? What reaction would my grandmother and the other church mothers have received if, while they were passing out tracts, they had asked not "Are you saved?" but "Are you safe?"

Someone facing domestic violence wants to be safe. Someone dealing with schoolyard bullies needs to feel safe. Someone caught up in gang violence is praying to be safe. The question of safety is a pressing human need that transcends any particular religious tradition. And while "Are you saved by the blood of Jesus?" is a question that Christians may ask, Christians are commanded to care about the very real forces of danger, destruction, and disease that prevent anyone from being safe, whole, and free.

True salvation is a heavy weight, and wholeness is no trifling matter. Authentic salvation moves beyond your individual spiritual and physical health and encompasses all those around you. When I am spiritually and physically well, and when I am spiritually and physically safe, I have a responsibility to work so that other communities, peoples, and cultures can also be made safe and whole. Far too many of us are broken or in despair or unhealthy. Far too many of us are neither whole nor safe. We are scared to offer help to the person on the side of the road. And we are fearful of being the vulnerable person in need of help. We feel unsafe in reaching outside our usual boundaries, anxious that we will be misunderstood, misinterpreted, and maligned. We want salvation, but just for the people with whom we agree. We want safety, but just for the community in which we live.

True salvation and healing for the soul are only possible when love overshadows fear, when we embrace God's saving work more out of love for our neighbor than out of fear of hell and damnation.

9 Valley of the Shadow of Whiteness

Every valley shall be exalted, and every mountain and hill shall be made low: and the crooked shall be made straight, and the rough places plain. And the glory of the Lord shall be revealed, and all flesh shall see it together.

—ISAIAH 40:4–5

The much-too-expensive hardcover book was a reward for promises kept. My daughter had delivered on her grades, and now I needed to keep my half of the bargain and deliver the newly released volume in a never-ending series of fantasy novels. That is why I found myself with my then middle school–aged daughter at our local independent retailer.

When my daughter and I entered the bookstore, the reaction was immediate. Before we could even navigate around the first set of displays, we were being followed. No greeting had been offered, just a quick step from behind the counter to follow us. At one point, the worker was so close behind us that I could smell on her breath the food she had been eating before we entered the store. I took a deep breath and stopped dead in my tracks. She bumped into me.

"Can I help you?" she asked at last. "No thank you. We're just browsing," I responded. But as she continued to follow us, the only two customers in the store on a sunny weekday afternoon, I was torn between my deep anger and humiliation and my promise to my child. Holding my daughter's hand, I said brightly, "Let's come back another day. We can get some ice cream first." And I engulfed her small brown body in my own, leading her to the door as quickly as I could.

My daughter took one look at my face when I suggested we leave, and she did not say a word. Little brown girls grow up to be unusually intuitive to their mothers' pain. And she knew I always kept my promises.

Please do not tell a grown Black woman who has shopped throughout the world that she does not know when she is being racially profiled. Do not suggest that the color of her skin has not elicited a threat. Do not dismiss her stories of being treated preemptively like a criminal and a trespasser. It did not matter that there was not one thing in that store I could not afford; it did not matter that absolutely no one else was in the store. We were being followed because we were perceived as potential thieves. We were being followed because we are Black.

Even now, years later, I can feel the sting of this woman's hot breath on the back of my neck as she followed us. We may have only been in that store for three or four minutes, but for me, her breath encapsulates a lifetime of indignities of living while Black in the valley of the shadow of whiteness.

Before we reached the door that day, still accompanied by our hostile shadow, another mother-and-daughter pair entered. Our two girls immediately recognized each other from school and began to excitedly chat. After we greeted each other, this mother began to usher her daughter around the store, taking much the same path as my daughter and I had done only moments earlier. But there was no accompanying shadow for them. The shadow remained with us until we physically exited the door, while our white doppelgängers were allowed to browse in peace. Stepping into the fresh air outside, I watched from the window as our shadow retreated to her neglected lunch at the cash register. I watched while the other mother and daughter shopped without her piercing gaze.

Only days later did I realize how much this white mother and daughter duo mirrored me and my daughter. The mother and I were both professors, and our daughters were in the same grade at the same school. Had anyone been looking at the four of us in that moment, they could not have perceived the gap that separated us. But the valley between whiteness and Blackness proved to be a gap in which one mother and daughter pair were presumed guilty and the other mother and daughter were presumed innocent.

The valley of the shadow of whiteness is a place in which whiteness is normative and righteous. This valley is not merely the place of flawed race relationships, racialized disparities, or the mind-numbing racism of this country; it is also a place justified and sustained by Christian theology. A belief in the inherent goodness of whiteness as a construct easily morphs into a belief of the superiority of white people and the denigration of all others. This valley of the shadow of whiteness is reflected in the music, sermons, and rhetoric of Christian churches. I am increasingly convinced that the only way to bridge the valley and step outside of the shadows is to abandon the elevation of whiteness, metaphorical and literal. This is important in all our discourse, but particularly in the language of the church.

There are some songs that I no longer sing even though they were staples in my childhood and remain popular in worship services today. I no longer sing songs that petition God to wash me whiter than snow. As much as I love "Nothing but the Blood of Jesus," my mouth can no longer echo the sentiment "Oh! precious is the flow / That makes me white as snow." As much as I love the Mississippi Mass Choir's version of "Jesus Paid It All," the lyrics "Sin had left a crimson stain / He washed me white as snow" are no longer words my heart can sing. Likewise, I no longer sing songs that call on God to be "master" and me a "slave"; despite the sonic beauty of "I Love My Master," the lyrics "I love my Master, and I will not go out free" will no longer pass my lips.

I understand the metaphorical and theological nature of these songs. That one can be washed in the blood of Jesus and still be "clean" is a powerful symbol for the work of atonement. The image of being slaves to God and calling on God as "master" suggests that we cast off the yoke of sin and carnality and willingly embrace a heavenly authority. These songs are "biblical" inasmuch as they echo and affirm scriptural texts. Psalm 51 is a beautiful passage in which the repentant David asks for forgiveness, to be washed white as snow, for his many transgressions. Romans 6 includes the apostle Paul's urging to followers of Christ to be slaves to righteousness, to be slaves to God, thus reaping the benefits of holiness and eternal life.

Yet despite their biblical foundation, I can no longer sing these songs. These metaphors and symbols undercut the very essence of the God in whom I put my trust. The idea that whiteness represents purity and godliness, while Blackness represents sinfulness, carnality, and impurity, supports a dichotomy that has been one of the most destructive forces on earth. I do not need to be metaphorically or theologically stripped of my Blackness in order to participate in the beloved community of God. Every time we sing songs that affirm this, we are dehumanizing those whose Blackness is an essential part of who they are. History bears witness to the cultural, political, and religious attempts to strip those who are Black of their literal skin as well as of their citizenship, birthright, and place in God's family. For my own spiritual well-being, I have had to let go of those songs that ask me to don a "whiteface"—I cannot participate in a kind of reverse minstrelsy in praise of God.

The same applies to all the master and slave songs, particularly the hymns written and popularized during the slave trade and era of enslavement. I understand the intent of the hymn writers: by identifying with the all-encompassing, life-and-death nature of slavery, they sought to affirm God as a benevolent ruler whose yoke was easy and whose burden was light. The believer could be a "slave" to this kind, gentle, and perfect "master," who was completely contrary to sinful human slaveowners. But again, while I understand the metaphor, I reject it. As a descendant of enslaved persons, I cannot easily dismiss the utter depravity of slavery. My generational memory will not allow me to forget the chains of physical and psychological bondage, which rendered human beings as property and tore families asunder—chains that linger with us today. For those with no direct knowledge of enslavement, terms such as *master* and *slave* are merely words, seemingly devoid of any particular historical context. But they are not words I can ever sing again or use to refer to my own relationship with God. As an African American Christian, I traverse the valley of the shadow of whiteness when Blackness is demeaned and only associated with sin and death.

My faith has liberated me. It has set me free, and I am free indeed. Mine is not a faith that requires me to be white as snow in order to be saved, because my Black body is lovingly made in God's image. It is not a faith that requires me to embrace the yoke of slavery, because the captives have already been set free. The music of my heart is a song of liberation, a song in which I am loved and cherished. The music of my heart cannot perpetuate stereotypes and imagery that harm or denigrate God's people.

Our limited human language fails in our efforts to describe God and God's love for us. We struggle to articulate the complexities of our faith, and so we draw on imagery from ordinary life to explain the extraordinary. We grope for words, sensing our inadequacy to summarize the mysteries of the faith. Yet it is problematic when symbolic language—Blackness and whiteness, master and slave, soldier and battle—become the default without any acknowledgment that there are real people and weighty historical context underneath the metaphors.

Christians often use military language to describe God and God's plan for the world—conquering the heart of the unbeliever, penetrating the mission field, and being soldiers in God's army. Battlefield imagery, combat terms, and martial talk are often used to urge Christians to remember the Great Commission: to go into the world and preach the gospel. Yet war is all too real, and the repercussions of war are all too deadly. There are soldiers who defend the front line, but there are also soldiers who have raped and looted on behalf of their army. There are far too many armed conflicts around the globe that are destroying families, cultural groups, and the earth itself. And in places where Christianity has "conquered" with the sword, the seeds of enmity and discord against the Christian world have also been sown. For far too many of our neighbors, military imagery means death, destruction, loss, and hate, even if sung to the tune of "Onward, Christian Soldiers."

Words matter. Symbols are heavy, laden with meaning and history. If whiteness becomes a stand-in for all things holy and pure, it is only a short leap to whiteness being equivalent to godliness. As Christians, we must grapple with a text whose very translation often pits Blackness and whiteness in an eternal struggle. We must walk through the valley of the shadow of whiteness found in the very book we love and revere.

An occupational hazard that comes along with being a scholar of religion is that you receive a lot of Bibles as gifts. On every occasion—birthdays and holidays, graduations or life celebrations—some well-meaning, kind person has given me a Bible as a present. I understand the thought process: "Here is someone who makes her living teaching about religion. Surely she would enjoy a Bible!"

So I now have every version of the Bible under the sun. I have Bibles with the Apocrypha and those without it. I have Bibles that include the "lost books" of the Gospel. I have some with the words of Jesus in red font, others with multiple color highlights. Some in my collection include commentary, maps, and concordances. Some are engraved with my name in gold leaf; others have the clearance price tags still on the cover. I have leather-bound Bibles, hardcover Bibles, paperback Bibles, and three-ring-binder Bibles. I have copies in Spanish and in Gullah and in every translation possible: the Message Bible, the King James Version, the new and revised version of the New Revised Version, and so on.

When I was growing up, we had a large family Bible, in which generations of our family history was recorded. This book occupied a special place in the living room, where it was regularly dusted and loved. Births, deaths, and marriages that took place before African Americans could receive official records of these events are all recorded in that book. I grew up with church folks who taught me to love the Bible with all my heart and to care for it with my hands. As a child, you learned to treat the Bible with respect and reverence. Raised in the Black church tradition, I had a particular notion of God literally dwelling within its pages; the Word was God and so the words of the text were sacred, and the book that contained these sacred words was a holy thing. Bibles were read, but carefully. They were never placed on the floor or treated as coasters. They were never subjected to the ravages of other well-read books—never tossed on the couch or casually left in the car or on a chair.

The Bible I now use on a regular basis is a well-worn affair. Despite all these gifts of Bibles, I am deeply attached to one edition, which accompanies me everywhere. This particular edition has been the source of my devotional life. Its pages are worn and tattered. There are notes in the margins and highlights of favorite passages. I have written in it, both exclamations of joy and questions of unbelief. It is the Bible that has traveled with me. I have turned to this book in joy and in frustration, and it has caught many tears that I have shed. And despite its age, I am not ready to retire its worn, well-thumbed pages.

My love of the text, however, does not blind me to its misuse and abuse. My love for the tattered pages of my own well-worn Bible does not negate the harm done in God's name and justified with the pages of this book. African American theologian and mystic Howard Thurman taught me that a critical reading—a hermeneutic of suspicion—was necessary for a genuine understanding of the Good Book.

Thurman (1899–1981) came to his knowledge of God in his grandmother's house. Mrs. Nancy Ambrose had been born during enslavement, and she took on the task of raising him after his mother's early death. In his groundbreaking work *Jesus and the Disinherited*, Thurman remembers:

> My regular chore was to do all of the reading for my grandmother—she could neither read nor write. Two or three times a week I read the Bible aloud to her. I was deeply impressed by the fact that she was most particular about the choice of Scripture. For instance, I might read many of the more devotional Psalms, some of Isaiah, the Gospels again and again. But the Pauline epistles, never—except, at long intervals, the thirteenth chapter of First Corinthians. . . .
>
> With a feeling of great temerity I asked her one day why it was that she would not let me read any of the Pauline letters. "During the days of slavery," she said, "the master's minister would occasionally hold services for the slaves. Old man McGhee was so mean that he would not let a Negro minister preach to his slaves. Always the white minister used as his text something from Paul. At least three or four times a year he used as a text: 'Slaves, be obedient to them that are your masters . . . as unto Christ.'

Then he would go on to show how it was God's will that we were slaves and how, if we were good and happy slaves, God would bless us. *I promised my Maker that if I ever learned to read and if freedom ever came, I would not read that part of the Bible.*" [italics mine]

When reading Thurman for the first time, I was struck by the audacity and courage of his grandmother in rejecting the parts of the Christian canon that had harmed her and justified her bondage. In fact, it was Nancy Ambrose—a woman who had known the bitterness of chattel slavery—who gave me permission to do what my own grandmother could not have done: find a way to love the Bible and to love my Blackness.

For Thurman's grandmother and for me, that means rejecting even sacred words that are not life-giving. It was this woman, who walked through the valley of the shadow of whiteness and came out on the other side, who helped me learn to affirm the scriptures as God-breathed and inspired while still being clear that fallible human hands had compiled and translated them. Nancy Ambrose, despite her illiteracy and lack of formal schooling, had the courage to do what ecumenical church councils and convenings had done 1,500 years earlier: decide what manner of God she was willing to worship and in whom she would place her trust. Having already known a human master, she rejected slaveholding language for her personal theology. She had been set free, and she was free indeed.

A grandmother theology contains generations of inherited wisdom. Thurman—civil rights activist, leader in various social justice movements, professor, theologian, philosopher, prolific author, and dean of Rankin Chapel at Howard University—credits his grandmother for the faith he received. He said that she inspired in him the belief that "the Creator of existence also created me."

Thurman was among the first generation of African Americans no longer born under the yoke of slavery. His grandmother, as well as his mother, had been born enslaved. If you were one generation removed from bondage for life, you would find it an extraordinary gift to hear the message that the very Creator of the universe also saw fit to create you. This confidence propelled Thurman to a lifetime of service for the cause of racial justice, not the least of which was serving as Martin Luther King Jr.'s spiritual advisor and teacher. There are civil rights we have today because Thurman's grandmother was bold enough to say that simply because it is in the Book does not mean that it is for me.

10 Sacraments

I might seem to be comparing something great and holy with a minor and ordinary thing, that is, love of God with mortal love. But I just don't see them as separate things at all. If we can be divinely fed with a morsel and divinely blessed with a touch, then the terrible pleasure we find in a particular face can certainly instruct us in the nature of the very grandest love.

—MARILYNNE ROBINSON, *GILEAD*

The writer of Baruch 5:1, an apocryphal book of Scripture, tells us, "Take off the garment of your sorrow and affliction, O Jerusalem, and put on forever the beauty of the glory from God." For the Hebrew people, wearing sackcloth, known as a "garment of affliction," was a sign of mourning and grief. That phrase—"garment of your sorrow and affliction"—echoed through my head as I was writing my first book on spiritual narratives written by people who were enslaved. I came across a reference to burlap grain bags that forever changed the way I thought about a garment of affliction.

Enslaved children were extremely vulnerable to disease and death due to both malnourishment and lack of clothing. This was true even in the warmth of the deepest parts of the South. To have an article of clothing—any clothing—was a relative luxury for babies and small children, who could not "earn" the cost of their upkeep. One writer describes the deprivation of his childhood in slavery and the incredible sacrifices his family made to feed, clothe, and shelter him: The enslaved children on the plantation where he was born were given burlap grain bags (literally, sackcloth) as Christmas presents to serve as clothing. People would make them into crude unisex dresses and shirts for toddlers and younger children. The writer describes the feeling of the heavy, rough material, which literally rubbed his skin raw. The discomfort was so intense that he preferred to be naked, despite his age and his sense of modesty.

In the autobiography he later published, this formerly enslaved man describes a sacrificial act by his older brother. For weeks, his brother wore the burlap grain bag as a shirt, using his skin and his very body as a softening agent. The elder sibling endured the pain of breaking in the raw and rough material, and only then did he pass on the softened garment to his younger sibling. The writer, who later became a Christian minister and prominent abolitionist, describes his older brother's wearing of the sackcloth as the greatest sacrifice he has ever known. The pain of his "garment of affliction" had been eased by someone willing to sacrifice his own comfort out of a sense of love.

While this account was among many other stories of sacrificial love I have written about within the slave narratives, the power and simplicity of this exchange has informed how I understand the power of sacrament. Simply put, the ritual exchange between these two brothers teaches that there is no sacrament without a sacrifice.

I used to think that the concept of sacrament applied to other churches and not my own Holiness-Pentecostal upbringing. The word *sacrament* conjured up the "smells and bells" of the Episcopal church, or the last rites of the Roman Catholic church, or the highly stylized Communion of the Presbyterian church. Coming of age in a church that felt highly improvisational—a place where the Holy Spirit could and did regularly alter any particular sense of ritual—I never particularly thought about the sacraments that had formed and shaped my theology. Yet I couldn't shake the story of a child in slavery enduring pain so that his younger brother did not have to face the same discomfort. This was the perfect example of how Christians are called to "bear the cross" for each other. This ritual was an outward sign of grace and love: the very meaning of sacrament.

Augustine of Hippo defined sacrament as the outward (or visible) sign of an inward (or invisible) grace, a sign of a sacred thing. Christians think about sacraments as those deliberate rituals, including baptism and the Eucharist, in which God is uniquely active. Sacraments involve tangible symbols—such as bread and wine—to convey a sacred meaning—such as the sacrificial work of Christ on the cross. Sacraments depend on the intention of the believer. You can regularly eat bread and drink wine at dinner, but that is not partaking of the Communion table. You can immerse yourself in a bathtub or pool or body of water, but that does not mean you have been baptized. Sacraments need deliberate intent, often in the presence of other believers, so that tangible symbols such as water, bread, or wine reflect an intangible and sacred reality. A pastor, priest, or leader often speaks instituting words at the beginning of each sacrament, such as "This is my body broken for you." These words, along with the symbols and the intentionality of the believer, transform the ordinary things of life into a sacred moment in glory of a holy God.

Once I understood the meaning of sacrament—once I grasped the power of that "visible form of invisible grace"—I realized that I had been surrounded by the sacramental all my life. Understanding the power of the presence of God in the ordinary stuff of daily living is contingent on understanding the sacrifice behind the sacrament. The sackcloth shirt worn by an enslaved child is not merely a garment but evidence of an older brother's sacrificial love. The things of life we often take for granted, even a piece of clothing, can be sacramental when they are a visible form of invisible grace.

***

I was ready to go. Although I was just sixteen, the time had come for me to leave the narrow path of my grandmother's house and head to college. This Friday-night church service was the last one I had to endure before my grandparents would deliver me to my school the very next day. That next day I would begin the life I had been eagerly anticipating my entire senior year of high school—a life, I had already determined, that would involve as little church as possible. After sixteen years of three to four services every week, I figured I had earned at least a four-year hiatus.

As I walked into the sanctuary, I could see the simple basins, pitchers, and towels already assembled near the altar. It was apparent that tonight's service would include foot washing, a tradition practiced in many Christian churches but most especially in those of the Holiness or Pentecostal variety. There never seemed to be a rhyme or reason to the schedule of foot washing at my childhood church. Whenever led by the Holy Spirit, the pastor would inform the church mothers to have things prepared to wash feet. Sometimes it was on a Tuesday, sometimes on a Friday, and sometimes even on a Sunday morning. Had I known that this last night at home was to be a foot-washing service, I may have tried harder to wiggle my way out of attending. I could have used the pretext of leaving for college the next day as a good excuse to not attend; I could have argued that I needed to stay home to pack. No teenager alive is interested in watching a group of elders wash each other's feet.

The service proceeded as usual, with singing and preaching and testimonies. There were prayers and praises and petitions. I played the tambourine half-heartedly, my thoughts filled with how extraordinary it was that I was leaving home the next day. I would be living away from this church and away from my grandparents for the first time in my life. Caught in my daydreams and fantasies of all the things I was going to do at college, I almost missed what was happening as the elder in charge of the service invited people to the foot washing.

Our congregation was old-school: women washed the feet of other women, and men washed the feet of other men. I was so uninterested in what I had seen hundreds of times before that I almost missed my grandmother telling me to go up to the altar. I was even more shocked when, once I got there, she indicated that I should take off my shoes and have my feet washed.

"Washed" is perhaps a misnomer. There is no actual washing, as everyone's feet are already clean. Even on a Friday night, you come dressed and pressed into the house of the Lord. In my grandmother's house, "washing" meant someone rubbing your skin with a scratchy washcloth in a tub filled with bubbles, as if to scrub away a layer off your skin. But at church, the foot-washing ritual generally just involves pouring water from the pitcher over feet that are in a basin and then patting them dry. I had done this before for many of the older women in our congregation, because as children in the church, we were taught by example. I had prepped the basins and the pitchers; I had washed and dried feet. I had learned to serve in every capacity in this church. But before this night, I never had my own feet washed.

As my grandmother indicated where I should sit, I internally resisted with every fiber of my being. I was ready to be done with church life and eager to move into what I thought of as a whole new world. That night, I simply could not imagine a scenario in which these church mothers, and my grandmother, should wash my feet. I could not imagine that these women I had known my whole life—women whose physical and spiritual food fed me, women who taught me to fear and tremble before God—were going to wash my feet. But I lowered myself into the chair, resigning myself to the fact that I could not escape the ritual before me.

Foot washing requires kneeling; it requires the posture of a servant. When Jesus washes his disciples' feet, they initially resist, not wanting the man they believed to be the Messiah, their king, to act as a mere servant, to perform a task that the lowliest of servants were called to perform. I had been taught to serve my elders, to come when they called or jump if they told me to jump. Nothing had prepared me for this moment in which they were to serve me.

As I sat there, with my grandmother kneeling before me, my sense of unworthiness brought tears to my eyes, and a spirit of repentance touched the very core of my being. The women who washed feet that night—including my grandmother, who washed mine—and the women who would later anoint my fore-head with oil in the sign of the cross were preparing to send me away to college and away from their influence. They were per-forming sacraments that were sacred to them: calling on God to protect me from the crown of my head to the soles of my feet. They used ordinary things—a towel, a pitcher, a basin, a vial of oil—to perform an extraordinary act of service, to create a hedge of protection around me before they sent me into the world.

That senior year of high school, I had attended prom, my first date with a boy; I had ridden in a limousine for the first time; I had traveled outside the country for the first time; and I had graduated at the top of my class. But those rites of pas-sage pale in comparison to the visceral memory I have of cool water pouring over my bare feet, the feeling of water between my naked, unpolished toes, and then the loving hands patting my feet dry. I imagine that some words were spoken and prayers were offered and scriptures were read, although I cannot remember. And I am sure the service continued, likely into the late hours of the night. I cannot recall. But this is the sacrament I have treasured all my life, the church mothers who taught me to cherish the act of washing feet.

In her poetry collection, *Rice*, African American poet Nikky Finney, a former colleague of mine, laments in her poem "Making Foots": "sore feet / standing on freedom lines / weary feet / stomping up a southern dust bowl march / simple feets / wanting just the chance." Her beautiful words articulate the sacrifice behind the sacrament of foot washing. The feet of my elders were the feet of civil rights protestors and former sharecroppers. They were the feet of domestic workers, factory laborers, and all those who earned a living on their feet. Standing, marching, protesting, picking, cleaning: hour after hour they were on their feet, in the cheap and ill-fitted shoes of poverty. It is no wonder that for many of them, foot washing became a sacrament. It became a way to symbolically cleanse the feet of laborers; to remind them that their earthly toil was secondary to their labor in the sacred vineyard; and to bless the most humble with a divine and holy touch.

I did not need to look outside the walls of my home or my church to see the sacramental in the lives of Black folks—those who, through their hugs and high fives, their pinching of baby cheeks and anointing with oil, sought to reveal the presence of God in all creation through their love for those in their families and communities. God's grace shows up in ordinary and extraordinary ways. This is what womanist theology taught me: to find God and sense of the sacred in the ordinary places Black women move, and live, and have our being.

One day years later, taking the train from New Jersey to Philadelphia, I was not thinking about God's grace but rather how to make the trip as quickly as possible in order to return to the work I had left undone in my office. I departed the train station and made my way through pregentrified Philadelphia on foot, destined for a house I had been to many times before. My great-great-aunt—or perhaps she was something like my third cousin once removed—lived in a neighborhood of cramped rowhouses and had done so for her ninety-plus years. The exact genealogy of the family ties remained unclear, but she was understood to be the oldest living matriarch in our family. I had been summoned to her home for the "baby ritual," subsequent to the birth of a fifth or sixth cousin, something we did for every baby born into our family.

"Baby ritual" makes it sound fancier than it was. Here's how it usually went: a scared father, holding his swaddled newborn and standing next to his confused wife, would hand over his brand-new baby to the seemingly ancient woman in a wheelchair. She would immediately unwrap the baby, who would inevitably cry when the onslaught of cool air hit their skin and who would continue wailing as both the blanket and the diaper were removed by frail hands. Our family matriarch would look at the baby, turn the naked baby around, and look again. Then, without a word, she would promptly and unceremoniously hand the baby back to the anxious parent—or any adult standing nearby—without having uttered a word. That was it. With the ritual over, the parents would reswaddle their precious gift, and the rest of us would go home. A few would stay after for the family dinner.

This time, I thought as I made my way on the train to Philadelphia, the ritual would be different. I was eager to tell everyone gathered about the research I had done in graduate school about baby rituals. Over the years, I had become intrigued as babies were presented and no one would even comment on why we had gathered. With a fresh doctorate in hand, I needed everyone to know exactly what we were doing, why we were doing it, and how it connected to traditional African rituals. I was excited to share my newfound knowledge and book smarts, having made the assumption that their silence equaled their ignorance.

I was especially eager to tell everyone what things we were doing wrong, what things we must have forgotten to do, and how this ritual really needed to be performed. In my mind, the baby ritual should have been a naming ceremony; there should have been an evocation of the ancestors; there should have been the presentation of gifts and offerings. Essentially, I thought our family baby ritual should be the stuff I had read about in textbooks: an American mirror of our African ancestry.

Greeting my second or third cousin, the new baby's grandmother, on the tiny front porch, I mentioned to her what I was going to share this time around. I told her why we needed to do things differently, how everyone needed to know why we had been gathering and performing this ritual for generations.

With much patience and wisdom, she imparted a measure of God's grace to me in that conversation on the front porch. She told me gently that the ninety-plus-year-old woman inside probably did not need the musings of newly minted PhD, whose ink had not even dried on her diploma. She noted that I seemed eager to have this moment conform to an arbitrary standard I had developed in my own mind without accounting for the generations of accumulated wisdom that made this act meaningful all by itself.

Argumentative in that way that only a new assistant professor can be, I kept making my case to her about African rituals and retentions. Why was there no African name given to the new baby? Why were there no sacred objects or clothing presented to the newborn? Why did our baby ritual seem like a budget version of the ones I had read about in graduate school?

She, in her experience and love of God, made the case for a sacrament: an ordinary sign of God's grace. Most of the parents who present their babies to our matriarch, she explained, are entrusting their newborns to someone else's care for the first time. They see a pair of frail hands and a fragile body, but they must have trust for those few moments that their child is in the hands of someone who will never do them any harm. The grace of God, she continued, is believing that, despite what you see with your natural eyes, a loving and silent Power will never do you any harm. The grace of God is believing that this ancient Presence sees you in your most vulnerable state. This ritual, this sacrament, she argued, was never about the baby but always about the new parents. It was about new, scared parents who needed to learn to trust God like never before.

And that was the moment I knew, without a doubt, that although I had learned so much in over twenty years of formal school, I had been surrounded all my life by gifted Black women theologians, even if the academy never knew of their existence.

In her novel *Gilead*, Marilynne Robinson writes, "I might seem to be comparing something great and holy with a minor and ordinary thing . . . but I just don't see them as separate things at all." My grandmother washing my feet, our family matriarch unswaddling a newborn baby—these are minor and ordinary things. Yet they have been great and holy things in my life, keeping me connected to a faith that I may have long ago abandoned if not for the minor and the ordinary.

Writing has become my sacrament, the most visible form of God's invisible grace for me. It is what has kept me connected to a faith I thought I would abandon as soon as I left home after high school. With the blank screen before me, I compose prayers and sermons. I write litanies and liturgies. I work through theories of systematic and womanist theology. Mostly, I retell the stories that have been given to me by great women of faith. With the blank screen before me, I talk to God. With the blank screen before me, I try to bring to life a living and breathing faith that has sustained generations of my forebearers, even as I challenge aspects of the faith that have failed me or caused me doubt.

The traditional sacraments of the Christian church are beautiful. Baptism and Communion and marriage and confirmation are all sacred rituals in which God is active and present. But God also shows up at a baby ritual in a rowhouse in Philadelphia, just like God shows up when the church mothers wash feet. God is not contained by the orthodoxy of our rituals. Instead, God is concerned with the righteousness of our hearts. The baptism performed in a creek in the backwoods of Alabama is no less worthy than the one performed in the baptismal pool of Notre Dame in Paris. I have learned that God is far less interested in our production than in our true proclamation of God's word.

I believe that God is far less interested in how we perform our sacraments than in our heart of sacrifice behind the act.

These days I carry a small vial of anointing oil in my purse everywhere I go. And while anointing with oil is a sacrament often performed in the sanctuary of the church, over the years I have had many reasons to anoint others with oil in the most random of places. Sometimes it is a personal request from a student or a friend; other times it is something I offer to those with whom I have prayed or who have shared the burdens of their heart with me. I remind the recipient that the oil itself is nothing special. It is perfectly ordinary, extra virgin olive oil in a small, portable vial. And I, the person who is laying hands on them, am a perfectly ordinary woman with no special powers or gifts. But in the moment when they ask for a blessing with oil, and in the moment in which I anoint their forehead, God is supernaturally present in this exchange of touch and belief.

We, the ordinary and the flawed, affirm and proclaim the power of an extraordinary and perfect God, even if we are sitting in the dining hall on campus or in the waiting room at the hospital. The beauty of a sacrament is that God meets us where we are, always offering grace and love in exchange for our imperfect and mundane human symbols. A loving older brother and a matriarch in a wheelchair are reflections of God's love on earth, visible and tangible vessels of unmerited grace.

11 How Can I Say Thanks?

And they lifted up their voices, and said, Jesus, Master, have mercy on us. And when he saw them, he said unto them, Go shew yourselves unto the priests. And it came to pass, that, as they went, they were cleansed.

—LUKE 17: 13–14

Ten people broken and ostracized. Ten people crying out for deliverance. Ten people cleansed by the power of the Great Physician. Ten people able to return to their homes and families. And only one returns to say thank you.

I remember being taught this story from Luke as a young girl in Sunday school, during the lesson about being thankful when someone does something kind to you. But this passage is not about the thank-you as much as it is about the returning and the remembering. In the story, only one of those healed returns to Jesus. He does not just say thank you; he throws himself at the feet of Jesus and cries out in a loud voice. This is not polite gratitude for a favor done. This is the cry of someone who has been restored to a healthy condition, a condition he thought unattainable.

Gratitude, real thankfulness, is a mental return to the moment of need—a physical, spiritual, or emotional need. You may have needed healing or you may have just needed a drink of water or a chair to sit on. Gratitude requires returning to that moment of need even after the need has been met. To be thankful for the water that quenched my thirst is to remember the moment in which I felt parched. And when I remember, I cannot help but express gratitude to the one who thought it not robbery to attend to my needs, however large or small. In that moment of thankfulness, I remember the sensation of thirst and am grateful for the one who has poured water into my cup.

I have been in all three positions articulated in the story from Luke. I have been the broken one in need of healing, who fails to return to my moment of need and to remember after I have been healed. Full of energy and new life, I have forgotten to acknowledge the source of my strength and say thank you. I have forgotten to send that email or that card to let someone know how they have blessed me. I have taken a gift for granted and walked away without a spirit of gratitude for the gift giver.

I have also been the one who has returned, throwing myself at the feet of those who have so richly blessed me. I have at times heeded my grandmother's advice to "give others their flowers while they are still living." Whether with real flowers or words of praise, I have at times remembered to return in gratitude to those teachers or neighbors or colleagues who have blessed my life even if they did not know it.

But nothing has humbled me more than to be on the receiving end of someone's gratitude. After a long season of pouring out pieces of my heart and soul, thinking no one understands or appreciates my efforts, I may receive a card or note or a visit with words of thanks. Tears flood my eyes when this happens, because at that moment I truly understand the power of gratitude. The recipient has been blessed, and their expression of gratitude humbles and blesses the gift giver.

It is this space of mutuality—giving and receiving, thanking and being thanked, returning and remembering—that we can truly appreciate the story of the one man with leprosy who returns with words of thanks. He is not only cleansed; in his expression of gratitude, we can locate his complete healing. The cleansing from the disease takes place after only a few words from the Healer. But the full healing of his mind and body happens when he acknowledges his need, gratitude, and love for the Divine One. Ten are cleansed, but only one, through remembrance and return, is made completely whole.

Yet there is another moment in this story that should give the careful reader pause. Jesus does not immediately heal the ten afflicted men. He tells them, while they are still in an "unclean" state, to go and show themselves to the priest, who has the authority to declare them free from disease and to reintegrate them into the larger society. The men are healed on the way. They have to operate by faith that somewhere, en route to their destination, their condition will miraculously change from "unclean" to "clean." They trust Jesus's words of healing enough to believe they will be made well even while on their way. Thus they can faithfully transgress the social boundaries that typically separate the "clean" and "unclean."

These facts confirm two important lessons I learned in my grandmother's house: Gratitude is connected to trust. And miracles are real.

⚙ ⚙ ⚙

I have hosted huge Thanksgiving Day dinners for at least a decade. It started with just a few family members, but these days, former and current students, academic colleagues, and lifelong friends come over. Easily fifty or so people attend. Some get a plate of food or dessert to go, as they move on to their next holiday stop. Others linger in the kitchen until cleanup, staying late into the night. The dinner is always a period of wonderful chaos, preceded by three straight days of cooking every dish from scratch. Everyone always thanks me profusely for the food and the invitation to fellowship. Yet I am fairly certain that I'm the most grateful person there. This holiday meal is my way of remembering the tables of my childhood, where I was fed and nurtured with food for the soul.

A child cannot fully know how they are being cared for and blessed, fed, and nurtured. You eat the food placed before you, and you absorb lessons you are not even aware are being taught. I simply trusted that my grandmother and the church mothers wanted the best for me, wanted more for me than they wanted for themselves. I had no way to express my gratitude when I was a child because I was unaware of the gifts of love, mercy, and grace that were extended to me.

It was only on the way to my own adult life that I began to grasp the profound wisdom I learned around dinner tables, in small Sunday-school classrooms, and in church basements. All those who grew up within the Black church—in places where African American people, under their own vine and fig tree, gather for worship—have experienced at least a portion of this wisdom. The Black church has been the spiritual gathering of people of African descent, those who found themselves a peculiar people, at home and yet perpetually foreigners. African Americans built for themselves spiritual homes in a nation in which they have been perpetually treated as strangers.

The Black church has been a place of refuge as the sons and daughters of enslaved persons and sharecroppers became priests and bishops and evangelists.

The Black church has been a physical sanctuary, with congregations housing fugitive slaves and serving as stops on the Underground Railroad.

The Black church took the songs, the field chants, the spirituals, and the blues and elevated them to sacred music. It created liturgies and litanies and art and drama that spoke to the heart and to the soul.

The Black church challenged slavery while praying on its knees and also standing upright. Pew by pew and denomination by denomination, Black churches advocated and agitated for freedom.

The Black church coordinated the migration efforts of African Americans leaving the South in search of the American dream. These same churches then provided havens when the dream was replaced with the reality of the American nightmare.

The Black church birthed and funded the largest and most effective grassroots political movement—the civil rights movement—which challenged Jim and Jane Crow, lynching, segregation, and voting restrictions.

This is the church into which I was born and that my grandmother and other church mothers bequeathed to me. How can I say thanks? How do I express my gratitude for a generational legacy that I am only now beginning to understand? What are the right words to express appreciation for the "somebodiness," as Martin Luther King Jr. calls it, that I learned at the feet of my elders? Are there words to convey the treasure I inherited from people who created a distinctly African American faith—a theology that consistently and unequivocally contested white dominance? How can I say thanks for a theology not just rooted in eschatological hope but focused on becoming the beloved community on earth as it will be in heaven?

As grateful as I am for this legacy of faith, I am also deeply concerned about the unrealized potential of the Black church I love so much. I lament the theological emptiness of some churches, which tell you just to "name it and claim it" without a fuller understanding of how God moves in the world. The theological emptiness of churches that ignore the crisis of intracommunity and intimate partner violence, offering little more than token thoughts and prayers to those who are hurting. The theological emptiness of churches in which women are restricted from serving in the pulpit and yet encouraged to give their last dollar. The theological emptiness of churches in which praise and worship music contains little more than clichéd platitudes. And the theological emptiness of the churches whose members drive into—and then quickly away from—the very communities of blight and decay in which the sanctuary is located.

The Black church has replicated the worst of patriarchal structures, misogyny, and discrimination. It has been the house of God for some even as it has failed to be a safe haven for many others. And I am left living in the tension: gratitude for what I have inherited, sadness at the unfinished work of what we can be.

In this place of tension, I must trust in God. I must trust that when we know better, we do better. I must trust that a new generation of believers knows enough of the history of the Black church to call forth her greatness. And I must trust that those of us with a heart of gratitude for the Black church and her gifts are also the ones who can hold her accountable for her failures. A justice-centered, theologically rigorous, people-affirming, life-giving, and Spirit-breathed church is possible because God is still in the blessing and miracle-working business.

Wednesday-night testimony services can seem endless to a young child. What is more monotonous than listening to adults talk—and hearing them say the same thing over and over again? During a regular Sunday-morning service, at least there is music, and dancing, and movement, and enthusiastic preaching. There's a packed house. On Wednesday nights, however, there are just a few of the saints in attendance, a few songs, and lots of testimonies. And more testimonies.

The testimonies follow a formula that you quickly learn. First someone gives honor to God and then greets, according to proper protocol, all the people of God's house. They may quote a favorite scripture or song that has encouraged them. There is usually a story about God's work in that individual's life or about God meeting a specific need. And sometimes there is an explicit request for prayer, usually in a particular area in which "the devil stays busy."

Every week, I heard stories of lives changed and worlds transformed. God was Healer and Provider. God was Way Maker and Mind Regulator. I listened to extraordinary stories of cancer healed and bills paid. God knit together broken bones and returned unrepentant children to their parents. God stopped evil bosses from firing people and miraculously created new jobs when old ones ceased to exist. The miracles that Jesus performed in my childhood church in Brooklyn echoed the miracles I read about in all the Gospels. If Jesus healed ten lepers almost two thousand years ago, Jesus could surely heal Deacon Walker's painful arthritis. Every testimony I heard confirmed that God was in the miracle-working business.

But it is not the miraculous stories that echo in my spirit today. Instead, I can still hear the testimonies of those who rejoiced in the God of the ordinary. A testimony service was a chance to simply thank God for waking you up in the morning and clothing you in your right mind. Sometimes the testimony was a simple "I'm so glad I'm here, in Jesus's name." Others testified that they were glad to be in the house of the Lord one more time. My favorite elder would simply say, "I was glad when they said unto me, let us go into the house of Lord"—and then he would sit down, not to say anything else for the rest of the service. I appreciated his brevity.

Years of sitting on a hard pew while listening to testimonies fostered an appreciation in me for the ordinary ways God shows up for God's people. It is a wonder to wake up in the morning, with one's mental faculties still intact. We should rejoice in the food on our table and the clothes on our backs. We must celebrate on behalf of fixed hearts and made-up minds.

I learned then, and I am slowly growing to appreciate now, that the ordinary things of God are also miracles. It is a miracle to love a church that may not be growing and appears to be dying, just as Jesus called dead things back to life. It is a miracle for the chicken and fish dinners cooked in church basements to fund a food pantry, just as Jesus fed the multitudes with a few loaves and fishes. It is a miracle that an institution that first worshipped in the hush harbors of enslavement grew to include cathedrals and congregations, just as Jesus promised to complete the work he first began.

The ordinary testimonies of ordinary church people are also miracles. Testimonies allow you to assert your humanity, your dignity, and your agency. In every testimony I heard while growing up, regardless of the particular subject, the speaker affirmed these three things:

Humanity: I exist, and I am uniquely made in God's image.

Dignity: My story matters, and the material and spiritual conditions of my life matter to God.

Agency: I choose to serve God.

While Deacon Walker's testimony was about God's supernatural healing, it was Deacon Walker himself who was actually the miracle. His survival—his very being—was the miracle. The dignified way he donned his hat and suit and faithfully arrived at the doors of the church where he had been a member for eighty-five years: that was a miracle. His willingness to serve God, even when wracked with pain, was the miracle. His successful flight from the terror of lynching in Oklahoma was the miracle.

Christians have been so conditioned to look to the stories of the Bible for evidence of God's miraculous work that we fail to appreciate the extraordinary in the commonplace and the everyday. I now understand the faith community that surrounded a young girl sitting quietly on hard church benches was a miracle. And the voices of a million angels cannot express my gratitude for the lessons taught, patience learned, and love given.

12 Notes on the State of Virginia

Ancestors never die till there is no one to call their names.
—AFRICAN PROVERB

Sadie, Earnestine, Mildred, Frances, Vivian, Beulah, Johnnie Mae, Hattie, Virginia, and Etta. These Southern-born but New York–made Black church women had weighty names. I am always startled to encounter a cherubic blond-haired and blue-eyed toddler bearing the same name as a seventy-year-old Black woman: Celia, Dinah, Harriet, Ruth, and Priscilla.

Of course, we dared not call any adults we knew by their first names. Before the first names of older Black women from my church and neighborhood would have been an honorific or title. In church, someone was Sister, Brother, Deacon, Elder,

Mother, or Pastor. At home, someone was Auntie, Uncle, Mr., or Mrs. These titles were rooted not in formality but in intimacy. They were not about artifice but about respect, which we were taught was the basis of the relationship between children and adults. These titles were also about granting dignity in a country that historically afforded very little to African Americans.

In Gadsden, Alabama, in June 1963, civil rights activist Mary Hamilton stood silently in a courtroom, having been arrested for a nonviolent protest. She refused to answer the prosecutor's questions until he called her "Miss Hamilton." She was jailed and held in contempt of court. Eventually her case landed before the Supreme Court, which, in *Hamilton v. Alabama*, rendered a final decision that no court could address Black witnesses differently than it addressed white ones. How and why you call someone's name has always mattered deeply to Black people.

Years ago, I began to incorporate the practice of calling my ancestors' names in my devotional life and also in my work as a scholar. I explicitly call the names of the dead, at least the names I know and to whom I am tied by flesh and blood. I also call on the ancestors from whom I am many generations removed and to whom I may not be biologically related. Like many African Americans, I can only trace my family lineage to a certain point, and I have more questions than answers about my actual family tree. So I include among my ancestors all peoples of African descent throughout the diaspora, caught in the tangled web of transatlantic slavery and its afterlives.

There is power in ancestral memory and ancestral veneration. As a Christian, I love the concept of a "great cloud of witnesses" affirmed by my faith. Yet my great cloud of ancestral witnesses extends far beyond the faithful names called in the Christian "hall of fame" of Hebrews 11. Something deeper and stronger happens when, in addition to the biblical heroes, we name our ancestors. I feel tied to the ancestors, known and unknown, and the faith that sustained their lives. I feel comforted in the knowledge that there are ancestors, not even related to me by blood, who have walked the path I am now walking. I believe that my name is on an ancestor's lips—that even now, someone who has gone before is praying for me and on my behalf. I believe that I have inherited their stories and their songs and that I am obliged to share them with the next generation. These beliefs bring me comfort and joy.

Some Christians are deeply afraid of other cultures and religious traditions in which worship of the ancestors is routine. Anti-Black sentiment, even within African American Christian spaces, makes many deeply suspicious of African practices that invoke the presence of ancestors. As a Black woman whose family history has been disrupted by the institution of slavery, I find that naming, remembering, and calling upon the ancestors is a profound act—not of worship but of veneration. It cultivates in me a deep respect for my forebearers and awe at their wisdom and strength. Calling upon the ancestors is about memory: remembering how I am connected to a web of humanity that does not end when our bodies have returned to dust. I want to excavate these ancestral memories, to listen as voices speak to my heart across time and distance, to pay attention to the stories of people whose voices were silenced when they were alive. I feel the presence of these ancestors encouraging me to speak truth in places and spaces they were never allowed to enter.

My ancestors include those exiled by slavery, war, and genocide, forever seeking but never finding a place that feels like home. My ancestors include those who worshipped the sun, the moon, or the very earth itself, pouring out libations in praise and awe of creation's beauty. My ancestors include those whose bodies now rest on the bottom of the Atlantic Ocean, never having survived the perilous journey to the "New World." My ancestors include those who fought their chains and those who stoically endured theirs. They may have arrived in 1619, when some twenty or more Africans arrived at Point Comfort, Virginia, as human beings only to die as chattel slaves. Whoever they were, I am linked to them. I want to remember them, and I want to honor them. And I cannot allow xenophobia, racism, or fear of the other to keep me from remembering their stories and honoring their lives.

I often begin my classes on African American religious history with a list of names, but not of the great people of the

Christian tradition or the churches and institutions that have contributed to this legacy of faith. No—I begin with a list of the names of the cargo ships used to transport enslaved African people from the shores of one continent to the other. I read the names of these ships, sometimes with the names of the ship captains and in concert with the entity that sponsored each voyage.

I want my students to know that many of those who were enslaved first encountered the symbol of the cross flying on the flag of the ship that carried them to enslavement. My students need to know that there was a Portuguese slaver's ship named *Bom Jesus do Triunfo* and a Spanish slaver's named *Jesús y Espíritu Santo*—among many others—that sailed with the explicit purpose of enslaving other human beings. These are the names that history records and remembers: captains, slave owners, financial companies, churches, and denominations that earned their wealth by trafficking African bodies. There are no records of the names of those whose bones now litter the ocean, some choosing to jump to their deaths in acts of defiance, others thrown overboard when ill or dead, treated like debris. To call on the names of my ancestors is to never forget the horror they faced. We need to speak the names of these witnesses who are not found in the biblical text or the history books. We need to speak their names because the ancestors never die unless we fail to remember them.

Speak the name of that teacher who inspired you. Speak the name of the grandmother who raised you. Speak the name of the neighbor who always had a kind word for you. Speak the names of those aunties who schooled you. Speak the names of those you love and have never forgotten. And when you cannot speak their names—when you do not even know their names—whisper a prayer of thanks that your life, with all its failures and successes, may be your ancestors' wildest dream.

❈ ❈ ❈

There are far more funerals than baptisms. That is the current reality of the American Christian church. Pastors must commit bodies to the ground, week after week, as aging congregations grapple with their mortality and the lack of membership among the young. In the best of circumstances, the deceased has lived a long life and has transitioned peacefully. But too many pastors, particularly African American pastors, face the reality of funeralizing the very young: those who have died violently, whose lives are cut short by the ravages of disease, who died at the hands of those sworn to protect them. How do you comfort a grieving Black mother whose only son has been killed by the police? What words do you offer a community when the scourge of gun violence kills elementary school children walking home in the middle of the afternoon? What can you say to Black parents whose greatest fear is that their child will not live long enough to graduate from high school?

I wonder whether we should bring back the tradition of the mourning women of Jeremiah 9:17: "Call for the mourning women, that they may come; And send for skillful wailing women, that they may come." In the biblical context, women worked as professional mourners, particularly for the wealthy. And throughout world history, in almost every religion and culture, women have served as transmitters of lament. Black women, in particular, have a reservoir of pain and tears from which to draw. We have generations of trauma from which to pull in our capacity as "mourning women." Our laments are both corporate and personal, but there is often no safe space in which to share our pain. The larger world believes that Black women are so accustomed to tragedy—that we are impervious to even physical pain—that our personal losses barely register with other people.

As a graduate student, I read Thomas Jefferson's *Notes on the State of Virginia* for the first time. In the section in which Jefferson delineates his perception of the differences between enslaved persons and white citizens, he writes that the griefs of members of the Negro race are "transient." Their afflictions, he claims, "which render it doubtful whether heaven has given life to us in mercy or in wrath, are less felt, and sooner forgotten with them."

I closed my book after reading those words. It was a cold and snowy winter day, typical for Ithaca, New York, and I sat and stared out the window of the library for a long time. I wasn't surprised by Jefferson's racist words; I knew too much about the lives and history of the founding fathers of this nation to ever be shocked by their heinous acts and unmitigated support for the brutality of enslavement. But his words about grief and transience took me immediately to a place of personal loss, a place from which I had long tried to escape.

⁕⁕⁕

I am sitting at my grandmother's funeral, thinking about the phone call that upended my world. The all-too-quick death. The train ride back to New York City. My entire world transformed overnight. I am unable to feel the grief of the moment, exhausted from the unending tasks that fall on my too-young shoulders. There is no one else left; they are all gone. I am all she had left, the last of this family line. I cannot cry because I fear that if I were to begin, I would never stop.

And so I sit in the front row of the church, a place I have known for years, surrounded by people I have not seen since I finished high school, and I am frozen in time. I am looking at the funeral program in my hand, reading an obituary I scarcely remember writing and staring at a picture that I do not ever remember seeing. And while the eulogist is preaching this final sermon, he calls my grandmother's name. I look up because he has called her Virginia.

My grandmother's name is Vivian.

I look swiftly to my right and to my left, a bit frantic. Did anyone else hear him call my grandmother by the wrong name? I stare, once again, at the program I have in my hand and the obituary I wrote myself, to confirm that her name is printed correctly. Yes, her whole beautiful name is there. I shake my head, determined to clear a mind that I know is clouded with grief. Maybe I heard him wrong.

There is no way that he said the wrong name. There is no way that you get something like that wrong at this time and in this place. And then the minister repeats himself. Four times he calls what he believes is the right name, and four times he fails. Four times he calls the name of some strong Southern woman—Virginia—who is surely someone else's beloved grandmother. But it is not the name of the one I know and love.

The first time I am able to cry is after the funeral, when I attempt, through heaving sobs, to explain to anyone who will listen that the preacher never said the right name. Only then do I truly begin to grieve the death of the woman who raised me and loved me. Kindhearted people attempt to explain to me that the preacher simply made a mistake, that he certainly meant no personal disrespect to me or my grandmother. I am left unable to explain in rational terms why this second blow, calling my grandmother by the wrong name, wounds me as deeply as the news of her death.

In my mind I am back in that library in Ithaca, New York, sitting with the absurdity of Jefferson's idea that grief for Black people is transient. I have been grieving my whole life. I have been wondering when the pain of so much loss will stop. I keep asking myself when my decades of grief will finally come to an end. When will the hole and empty space in my heart ever be filled? The clichés of my faith have provided little comfort. God did not need another flower in the garden. God did not need another angel in heaven. No good came out of my loss, and it was far more than I could bear.

I sit with the stark reality that you cannot escape grief. Grief will come for you and change your entire world. Grief will change your name, change your address, and change your sense of who you are. No accomplishment, no title, no honorific, no degree will alter the reality of my identity as a motherless child.

※ ※ ※

In anticipation of Easter, churches prepare for one of the busiest Sundays of the year, when the parking lots will be filled and the pews will be overflowing. Even people who do not normally attend church often find their way to a sanctuary on Easter morning to share in the triumphant message: "He is risen." For Christians, those words stir something deep within our souls. "He is risen, indeed!" is the joyous refrain we offer to the message of

Christ's defeat of death. In the Christian calendar, every day of Holy Week has a precious meaning. On Maundy Thursday, we remember the Last Supper of Jesus and his disciples. On Good Friday, we turn our focus to the passion of Christ and the suffering on the cross. And on Easter Sunday, we declare the victory of the Risen Savior.

But we often forget about Holy Saturday. Holy Saturday is perhaps the most important day of this sacred week because it is the day we must sit with death and grief as integral parts of our faith. Holy Saturday is the silence of a period that straddles death and life; it is the silence of work done and yet unfinished. The crucifixion has taken place, but the resurrection is still an impossible dream. Holy Saturday is the space between mourning and rejoicing; it is a time in which death has not yet been defeated, and victory cannot yet be proclaimed. The wailing women have mourned, and yet the first women who will receive the good news have yet to hear about the extraordinary turn of events. Holy Saturday is a time of doubt and unbelief. It is a time of a descent into hell, a time of loneliness and abandonment. The Anointed One has left his people, and they are uncertain and confused as to whether he was who he said he was. Holy Saturday forces us to pause, to not rush into the celebration to come. We cannot declare "He is risen" without dealing with the reality of death and grief and loss. How will you live when there is not yet the promise of resurrection?

Many of us spend quite a bit of our time in this "in-between" space that Holy Saturday represents: struggling with doubt, struggling with hell on earth, and struggling with work insistent and yet unfinished. We live in the space of justice delayed and justice denied. We live in the space of dreams deferred and dreams deterred. We cannot concede defeat, nor can we declare victory. It is a time in which God seems absent or silent. It is the pinnacle of all the times that we, with the man in Mark 9, cry, "Lord, I believe; help thou mine unbelief."

Holy Saturday is the tomb of parents mourning the deaths of their murdered children, with no hope that justice will prevail. Holy Saturday is the tomb of families at the borders who must choose between uncertain life or inevitable death. Holy Saturday is the tomb of those holding a vigil at a loved one's bed in hospice. Holy Saturday is the tomb of a mother who must choose between feeding her babies or paying the rent. Holy Saturday is the tomb of barren wombs, lack of love and healthy touch, and few choices for the future. Holy Saturday is the place where hope unborn has died.

There is a ritual in some churches that commemorate Holy Saturday, usually a late evening service. The parishioners arrive quietly, and the person leading the service blows out any candles that may be lit and turns off all the lights in the building. The congregation sits together for several hours, waiting, in silence but with great expectation, for the coming dawn. Sometimes there is an empty coffin present at the altar. It is a powerful worship experience to simply sit with death and all of the various representations of death: doubt, fear, loneliness, disbelief, and weariness. You know that the dawn will come, that the lights will be turned back on and the candles relit. But sitting in the silence of Holy Saturday prepares your heart for a resurrection and a rebirth, even if that hope feels long delayed.

Despite the losses I have endured, I have very few words to offer others who are also going through grief and loss. All I have is a mustard seed of faith that even when things are at their dimmest, light will surely come and illuminate the darkness. Even in the silence, a voice can speak words of comfort. Even in the presence of death, a new circle of life has already begun.

Like everyone whose life has been shifted, changed, and transformed by grief, I wait in the silence and in the stillness to hear the voice that says to me in the midnight hour, "Lo, I am with you always, even until the end of the age."

Afterword by a Daughter

As far as I know, I've only been to Brooklyn once. I must have been somewhere around ten years old—long enough ago that I can only remember a few details about the trip to New York with my mother. To me, those things seemed no different from details of the dozens of other trips we've taken together.

I don't recall what season it was. Something about the gray concrete surrounding tall buildings overwhelmed any perception of temperature. My mother told me that this was the building she had lived in when she was growing up and that she hadn't paid it a visit in a while. I remember her taking a piece of notebook paper, a letter, and folding it up. She must have written it before we left home. And I now wonder whether that was the entire purpose of our visit to Brooklyn. My mother folded up that piece of paper and put it in one of those plant holders outside the lobby of this tall apartment building that we never entered. The plant, evergreen, said nothing.

My first thought was: *Isn't that littering?* Was that all I could come up with? Did I say it aloud? Or did I just think it as my mother collected herself? She took my hand in hers as we left. She was a little more quiet than usual. Or maybe I sensed that it wasn't the time to ask questions.

I wondered what was in the letter she wrote and left in a planter in Brooklyn. Who was she writing?

I don't know whether she knows that I have this memory. I never thought much of it until I really had to think about inheritance, identity, roots. When we had to do family tree projects in elementary school, I was frustrated by all the missing branches that my mother did not know. Eventually I decided that I had my mother and I was fine; what else did I need?

It's only recently that I've been trying to peel back the layers. I never met my great-grandmother, but it's clear that she still lives within my mother. The way my mother meticulously explains the words of wisdom given to her as a young girl, her endless quests in the kitchen to re-create a pie that she can't finish alone and that she knows I won't eat, her attempts to teach me to play the tambourine all point back to a woman who would otherwise be a mystery to me. She lives in my mother. And that means she must live in me.

Truth be told, the stories my mother has shared with me have made me cry more than they've made me laugh. So many are about loss. I think there's something about being a daughter that makes you oblivious to your mother as an individual. I forget that my mother lived years and years before I was even a thought. I only know my life with her in it, and I know that's how she felt about her grandparents before she went off to college.

It's strange to think that in just a few years, I'll be the one graduating, and my life will really start to change. One day I'll bring my mother grandchildren that she can fawn over. She'll tell them stories about her life, and about mine. She'll teach them to bake pies in her kitchen. She'll tell them all about the chaotic preparation on Thanksgiving mornings as we fed dozens of students and family members from near and far. She'll tell them what I could never express about a mother's love. And I hope they will listen.

—Ally, Yolanda's daughter and Vivian's great-granddaughter

Acknowledgments

My love and gratitude to Keri Day, Myriam Exumé, Melissa Harris-Perry, Renee Harrison, Meta Jones, Frank Lance, Ally Stonum, Eric Williams, and Maggie Womack. And for all the amazing students it has been my privilege to teach and to mentor, thank you for allowing me to share my stories with you.

Notes

Chapter 1

page 1: Pauli Murray, "Nazarene," in *Dark Testament and Other Poems* (New York: Liveright, 2018), 65.

page 2: James Baldwin, *The Fire Next Time* (New York: Dial Press, 1963), 63.

page 14: Frederick Whitfield, "Oh How I Love Jesus," in *Sacred Poems and Prose* (W. Walker & Sons, 1861), 8.

Chapter 2

page 5: Toni Morrison, *Beloved* (New York: Alfred A. Knopf, 1987), 194.

page 20: Frederick Douglass, *The Autobiography of Frederick Douglass: An American Slave* (Boston: Anti-Slavery Office, 1845), 33.

page 22: Delores Williams, *Sisters in the Wilderness: The Challenge of Womanist God-Talk* (Maryknoll, NY: Orbis Press, 1993), 208–9.

page 23: Williams, *Sisters in the Wilderness*, 236.

page 28: Lucy Stone, 1856 testimony at the Margaret Garner trial, in Steven Weisenburger, *Modern Medea: A Family Story of Slavery and Child-Murder from the Old South* (New York: Hill and Wang, 1998), 173.

page 31: Baldwin, *The Fire Next Time*, 47

Chapter 3

page 33: Zora Neale Hurston, *Moses, Man of the Mountain* (New York: Amistad: 2010), 210–11.

Chapter 4

page 55: Langston Hughes, "Montage of a Dream Deferred." in *101 Great American Poems* (New York: Dover, 1998), 75.

page 57: Alice Walker, *In Search of Our Mothers' Gardens: Womanist Prose* (New York: Harcourt, 1983), xii.

Chapter 5

page 7: Audre Lorde, "The Transformation of Silence into Language and Action," in *Sister Outsider: Essays and Speeches* (Berkeley, CA: Crossing Press, 2007) 40–41.

Chapter 7

page 93: *Statistics reveal the crushing inequality*: For more on these figures, see "Weekend Read: Racism Is Killing Black Americans," Southern Poverty Law Center, July 19, 2019, https://tinyurl.com/ y9oaspck; "Fact Sheet: Black Women and the Wage Gap," National Partnership for Women & Families, March 2020, https://tinyurl. com/y9oaspck; and "Fact Sheet: The State of African American Women in the United States," Center for American Progress, November 7, 2013, https://tinyurl.com/hafsnty.

Chapter 8

page 101: Toni Cade Bambara, *The Salt Eaters* (New York: Random House, 1980), 10.

page 108: Lucille Clifton, "Why Some People Be Mad at Me Sometimes," in *The Collected Poems of Lucille Clifton 1965–2010* (Rochester, NY: BOA Editions Ltd., 2012), 262.

Chapter 9

page 123: Howard Thurman, *Jesus and the Disinherited* (Nashville: Abingdon-Cokesbury Press, 1949), 29–30.

Chapter 10

page 127: Marilynne Robinson, *Gilead* (New York: Farrar, Straus and Giroux, 2004), 204.

page 130: Augustine of Hippo, *City of God, Book X*, quoted in *The Routledge Companion to Religion and Popular Culture* (New York: Routledge, 2015), 180.

page 135: Nikky Finney, "Making Foots," in *Rice: Poems* (Evanston, IL: TriQuarterly Books, 2013), 42.

page XX: Robinson, *Gilead*, 204.

Chapter 11

page 149: Martin Luther King, "What Is Your Life's Blueprint?," in *A Time to Break Silence: The Essential Works of Martin Luther King, Jr., for Students* (Boston: Beacon Press, 2013).

Chapter 12

page 161: Thomas Jefferson, *Notes on the State of Virginia* (Boston: Wells and Lily, 1829), 145.